符号中国 SIGNS OF CHINA

紫砂壶

PURPLE CLAY POT

"符号中国"编写组 ◎ 编著

中央民族大学出版社
China Minzu University Press

图书在版编目(CIP)数据

紫砂壶：汉文、英文 / "符号中国"编写组编著. —— 北京：中央民族大学出版社, 2024.8

（符号中国）

ISBN 978-7-5660-2338-4

Ⅰ.①紫… Ⅱ.①符… Ⅲ.①紫砂陶—陶瓷茶具—介绍—中国—汉、英 Ⅳ.①K876.3

中国国家版本馆CIP数据核字（2024）第017446号

符号中国：紫砂壶 PURPLE CLAY POT

编　　著	"符号中国"编写组
策划编辑	沙　平
责任编辑	于秋颖
英文指导	李瑞清
英文编辑	邱　械
美术编辑	曹　娜　郑亚超　洪　涛
出版发行	中央民族大学出版社
	北京市海淀区中关村南大街27号　邮编：100081
	电话：（010）68472815（发行部）　传真：（010）68933757（发行部）
	（010）68932218（总编室）　　　　（010）68932447（办公室）
经 销 者	全国各地新华书店
印 刷 厂	北京兴星伟业印刷有限公司
开　　本	787 mm×1092 mm　1/16　印张：11
字　　数	152千字
版　　次	2024年8月第1版　2024年8月第1次印刷
书　　号	ISBN 978-7-5660-2338-4
定　　价	58.00元

版权所有　侵权必究

"符号中国"丛书编委会

唐兰东　巴哈提　杨国华　孟靖朝　赵秀琴

本册编写者

杨　冰

前言 Preface

在中国源远流长的历史中，品茶是一件雅事，并因此而形成了独特的茶文化。雅事必需雅器，而品茶的最佳雅器便是紫砂壶。紫砂壶被历代茶客奉为"茶具"之首，有"壶中壶"的美誉。

用紫砂泥烧制而成的紫砂壶，具有优良的宜茶性、透气性，能较好地吸附气体，吸收茶之香味，并能较长时间地保持茶味、茶香、茶色。

紫砂壶还是一件艺术品。一团泥

Tea appreciation has long been considered as an elegant practice in the history of Chinese tea culture and is to be partnered with a suitable tea ware. *Zisha* pot or Purple clay pot, much appreciated by tea drinkers and held up as the finest of all tea wares, fits the bill perfectly.

Made of purple clay, such a pot has a highly permeable texture and superior quality to absorb traces of tea, and to retain flavor, aroma and color in lengthy tea infusions.

It is also a work of art. A lump of clay, artistically hand-built by potters and burned at a high temperature, is fantastically transfigured into a piece of artwork. A profusion of artistic flavor and profound connotations of Chinese culture dwell on the extraction of materials, the design of teapot shape, as well as decoration and firing. Combining poetry, calligraphy, painting and

土，通过艺人之手，经过烈火高温，终成雅器。在这个过程中，材料提炼、造型设计、装饰、烧制等各个环节，都充满着艺术的气息，浸透着中国悠久的文化底蕴。经过数百年的发展，中国的紫砂产业日渐繁盛，并成为一种集诗词、书法、篆刻、绘画艺术为一体的独特文化。

爱壶则需养壶，紫砂壶使用越久，器身的色泽就越发光润，沏出来的茶也越发清香。相信读过此书，你也能爱上紫砂壶，享受茶与壶的世界。

seal carving, purple clay teaware — a unique cultural gem — has witnessed its increasing flourish in China after hundreds of years' development, and the purple clay industry eventually made a culture of itself.

Lovingly nursed, the purple clay pot grows lustrous and beautiful with age, and the tea infused in it becomes more aromatic. We hope this book will be of interest to you and bring you something appealing about these pots.

目录 Contents

紫砂文化八百年
The Culture of Purple Clay Pot—a Glorious History 001

"陶都"宜兴
Yixing—the Capital of Pottery 002

紫砂壶的历史
The History of Purple Clay Pot 008

紫砂壶与中国茶
Purple Clay Pot and Chinese Tea 024

紫砂壶的文化内涵
Cultural Connotations of Purple Clay Pot 041

造型之美
Beauty of Appearances 049

独一无二的泥中泥
Clay of Clay—a Unique Character 050

紫砂壶的结构
The Structure of Purple Clay Pot 059

紫砂壶的壶式
Shapes of Purple Clay Pot 068

工艺之美
Beauty of Craftsmanship 081

制作工艺
The Craftsmanship 082

烧制工艺
Techniques of Firing 086

装饰工艺
Decorative Methods 094

紫砂壶的款识
Inscriptions of Purple Clay Pot 111

妙手壶家
Masters of Teapot 117

供春
Gong Chun 118

时大彬
Shi Dabin (1573–1648) 121

惠孟臣 Hui Mengchen	123
陈鸣远 Chen Mingyuan	124
杨氏兄妹 The Yang Family	127
邵大亨 Shao Daheng	129
黄玉麟 Huang Yulin	131
程寿珍 Cheng Shouzhen	133
俞国良 Yu Guoliang (1874–1939)	134
裴石民 Pei Shimin	136
王寅春 Wang Yinchun (1897–1977)	138
朱可心 Zhu Kexin (1904–1986)	140
顾景舟 Gu Jingzhou (1915–1996)	142
蒋蓉 Jiang Rong (1919–2008)	144
徐氏兄弟 The Xu Brothers (1932/1937–)	147

李昌鸿
Li Changhong (1937–) 151

李碧芳
Li Bifang 153

吕尧臣
Lv Yaochen (1941–) 154

汪寅仙
Wang Yinxian (1943–2018) 156

周桂珍
Zhou Guizhen (1943–) 157

顾绍培
Gu Shaopei (1945–) 159

紫砂文化八百年
The Culture of Purple Clay Pot—a Glorious History

　　紫砂壶，不仅是茶具、艺术品，更是一种文化。紫砂壶从出现至今已有约八百年的历史，其造型多样，色泽古雅，具有良好的宜茶性和深厚的文化内涵，深受爱茶人士的喜爱，并逐渐成为人们收藏和把玩的艺术品。可以说，中国的茶文化因紫砂壶的出现而更加韵味深长。

Purple clay pot, with a history of eight hundred years, is not merely a tea ware or artwork but a culture of tea. Embracing a great variety of shapes and quaint luster, it has profound connotation and fits in well with tea, earning praise among tea enthusiasts, and further becomes the craftwork for both collection and appreciation. It can be said that the Chinese tea culture is further enhanced by the purple clay pot with more profound charm.

> "陶都"宜兴

在中国江苏省南部，有一座小城名叫"宜兴"。这是一座具有两千多年建城史和七千多年制陶史的文化名城，被誉为"千年陶都"。

宜陶之地

宜兴地处太湖流域，气候温和，雨量充沛，土壤肥沃，山秀水美，是江南著名的"鱼米之乡"。

宜兴是"宜陶之地"。历史上，宜兴的制陶业一直很发达，早在新石器时期，宜兴人就开始制陶。紫砂壶是用紫砂泥制成的，而宜兴是紫砂泥的唯一产地。此外，宜兴还盛产名茶，是中国久负盛名的古茶区之一，早在三国时期就因盛产"国山苑茶"而著称于江南。到了唐代，宜兴茶的名声甚至传到了宫廷，成为贡

> Yixing—the Capital of Pottery

Established about 2,000 years ago, the city of Yixing is located in the south of Jiangsu Province. with a history of more than 7000 years in pottery making, this cultural city is reputed as the "Pottery Capital of Thousand Years".

Yixing—a Suitable Place for Pottery Making

Lacated in the Taihu region, Yixing is blessed with a mild climate, plentiful rainfall, fertile land and beautiful mountains and rivers, which makes it the "Land of Milk and Money" in Jiangnan (regions south of the Yangtze River).

Yixing is a place most suitable for pottery making. Historically, Yixing's pottery industry has been well developed, and Yixing as a pottery town can be

• 宜兴竹海
Yixing Bamboo Forest

品。现如今，宜兴仍是江苏省最大的茶叶产区。那一片片的茶园，远远望去，青山逶迤，生机勃勃，犹如一片"茶的绿洲"。

千百年来，宜兴人一直以茶为伴，以陶为生。一把小小的泥壶，是许多宜兴人的整个世界。历史上的许多文人与宜兴紫砂艺术有着密切的关系，他们以定制、设计、撰铭、书篆等形式参与到紫砂壶的创作中，使其

traced far back to the Neolithic period. The purple clay pot is made of *Zisha Ni* or purple clay, which is only found in Yixing. In addition, Yixing is also famed for its tea. As one of the prestigious tea-producing areas in China, it was renowned in Jiangnan as early as the period of the Three Kingdoms (220-280) for the "*Guoshanyuan* Tea". In the Tang Dynasty (618-907), the increasing popularity of the tea from Yixing eventually made

由单纯的日用品变成了集金石雕塑、书画诗词于一身的艺术品，散发出浓厚的文化气息。

it a tribute to the imperial court. Up till now, Yixing is still the largest tea-producing area in Jiangsu Province where undulating hills are covered with rolling tea plantations, so vibrant and lively that they conjure up a green sea of tea.

For hundreds of years, tea has been a good company for Yixing natives while pottery has been their means to earn a living — a small clay pot means everything to many Yixing natives. In history, many literati were closely related to the art of Yixing purple clay. They got themselves involved in the creation of a purple clay pot in terms of commission, design, inscribing, calligraphy and seal. This makes an artwork combining epigraphy, sculpture, calligraphy, painting, poetry out of ordinary daily necessities, adding a strong cultural note to the teapot.

• 宜兴当地的人们在用紫砂做工艺品（图片提供:全景正片）
A Scene of Yixing Potters Making Purple Clay Products

宜兴"紫砂村"

宜兴有一个"紫砂村",原名"上袁村",是宜兴紫砂的发源地。紫砂村的不远处就是著名的黄龙山——紫砂泥的重要原产地之一。

从明清时期开始,紫砂村里的村民就开始世代制作紫砂壶。村子里绝大多数村民从事紫砂生产,并一直保持着传统的手工制作方式,几乎家家做紫砂、户户有作坊。

历史上,许多紫砂名师都诞生于紫砂村或曾在这里学艺,惠孟臣、陈鸣远、邵友兰、邵大亨、赵松亭、程寿珍、王寅春、顾景舟等制壶大师,皆出自此村。

"Purple Clay Village" of Yixing

The "Purple Clay Village", formerly known as "Shangyuan Village", is the birthplace of Yixing purple clay. Not far from it is the famous Huanglong Mountain, one of the key original producing places for purple clay.

As early as the Ming (1368-1644) and Qing (1616-1911) dynasties, villagers were engaged in making purple clay pot generation after generation. In this village, almost all households dealt with making of teapots and they had workshops of their own, the traditional hand-built technique being the dominant way.

Numerous great masters of purple clay pot were born in this village or had apprenticeship here, including Hui Mengchen, Chen Mingyuan, Shao Youlan, Shao Daheng, Zhao Songting, Cheng Shouzhen, Wang Yinchun, Gu Jingzhou, and others.

制陶窑场——丁蜀镇

"陶都是宜兴,陶业在丁蜀。"宜兴的制陶窑场大都集中在丁蜀镇,即丁山和蜀山所在之处。早在东汉时期,丁蜀镇就已经成为紫砂陶的制造中心了。之所以将窑场设置在这里,是因为丁蜀镇东临太湖,水陆交通十分便利,可以十

Dingshu Town—The Center of Pottery Kilns

"Yixing is the Capital of Pottery while pottery manufacturing dwells in Dingshu." Yixing pottery kilns mostly gathered in Dingshu Town where Dingshan and Shushan mountains are located. As early as the Eastern Han Dynasty (25-220), Dingshu Town became

分方便地把陶器产品运送出去。

　　走进丁蜀镇，你会发现，沿途的河道里满是装满坛、缸、壶、盆、钵等紫砂制品的大大小小的船只。河道两岸也摆满了这些货物；甚至一些房屋、牌楼也是用紫砂陶建成的。丁蜀镇的街道上，到处都是陶器店。无论是商铺的字号，房屋的大门，还是路灯的灯杆，甚至路边的垃圾箱，也大都以紫砂陶为原料。

　　任淦庭、顾景舟、蒋蓉等数十位紫砂艺术大师便出自丁蜀镇。最早的紫砂行业协会——宜兴紫砂同业公会、最早的紫砂工厂——宜兴

the manufacturing center of purple clay. This is because the town is on the east of Taihu Lake, where convenient land and water transportation greatly facilitate the shipping of pottery goods.

　　Entering the town, one will find the river is filled with boats of varied sizes, all loaded with purple clay products ranging from jars to tanks and pots to bowls. The banks of the river too, are occupied with these goods, even some houses and archways are made of purple clay. A large number of pottery shops line the edges of the streets in this town, and most of the shop plaques, gates of the housing, street light poles and dust bins, are built with this material.

• 丁蜀镇的跨河桥
Stone Arch Bridge in Dingshu Town

太湖风光
Sceneries of Taihu Lake

利永陶器商店、最早的紫砂职业学校——宜兴陶瓷职业学校，也都诞生在这里。而丁蜀镇的古南街，更是探寻古老紫砂文化的最佳去处。

1980年，位于丁蜀镇丁山北路50号的中国宜兴陶瓷博物馆建成。今天，它已发展成为我国规模最大的，也是唯一一座地方陶瓷博物馆，馆内陈列着万余种古今名陶，是中国灿烂陶文化的缩影。

如今的丁蜀镇，拥有数十家能够进行机械化生产的专业工厂，产品种类多达5000多种，年产量在4000万件以上，所生产的产品（以紫砂壶为主）远销海外50多个国家和地区，是真正意义上的陶瓷工业基地。

Ren Ganting, Gu Jingzhou and Jiang Rong, among dozens of great masters of purple clay ware, all came from Dingshu Town. The town also gave birth to these institutions: the Trade Association of Yixing Purple Clay, Liyong Pottery Shop of Yixing, Vocational School of Yixing Ceramics, all being the earliest of their kind. Further, Gunan Street of this town, once filled with pottery shops and studios in its heyday, is the best place for the taste of the ancient culture of purple clay.

Completed in 1980, China Yixing Ceramics Museum is located in Dingshan Beilu Street, Dingshu Town. After decades of development, the museum has grown into the largest and the only regional one around the country, in which over ten thousand ceramic masterworks past and present are on display, epitomizing the magnificent culture of Chinese ceramics.

Nowadays, Dingshu Town, as a ceramic industry base, has dozens of professional factories to carry out mechanized production, and yields as many as 5,000 kinds of products. With an annual output above 40 million pieces, their products (dominated by purple clay pots) are exported to over 50 countries and regions overseas.

紫砂壶
Purple Clay Pot

> 紫砂壶的历史

紫砂壶是在陶器制作的过程中出现的，至今已有八百年历史。在其发展过程中，紫砂壶从普通的茶具蜕变成了拥有无穷魅力的艺术品。

紫砂壶溯源

紫砂壶起源于北宋，在宋代文人的诗词中，可以看到许多"紫泥"的描述。如梅尧臣的《依韵和杜相公谢蔡君谟寄茶》："小石冷泉留早味，紫泥新品泛春华。"

这是迄今为止关于紫砂壶成为茶文化一部分的最早记录。

北宋越窑青瓷罐

> The History of Purple Clay Pot

The purple clay pot, a derivative of the process of pottery making, in its 800 years of development has been transformed from ordinary tea utensils into artworks of splendid charm.

The Origin

Purple clay pot was said to have originated in the Northern Song Dynasty (960-1127) as *Zini* or purple clay was found described by literati and scholars of this period in their poetry. Mei Yaochen — a famous poet, once wrote of the purple clay pot in a poem: "A tiny cute stoneware, coupled with cold

Yue Kiln Celadon Pot (Northern Song Dynasty, 960-1127)

宋代龙窑遗址
Site of Loong Kiln (Song Dynasty, 960-1279)

    1976 年，考古工作者在宜兴的丁蜀镇发掘出了一座长约10米、宽约1米的宋代古龙窑。龙窑中堆积有大量早期紫砂陶残器、废品。此外，人们又在南宋废井中发掘出了两件紫砂器皿。这两项重要发现，给紫砂壶始于北宋提供了有力的佐证。从器形来看，最初的紫砂壶是用来烹茶和煮茶的，这与当时社会盛行"斗茶"的习俗十分吻合。紫砂器在宋代只是崭露头角，与今天紫砂壶的样式不太相同，也没有达到如今紫砂壶在茶文化中享有的地位。

    明朝时，宜兴出现了一位在紫砂壶发展史上具有里程碑意义的人物——金沙寺僧，周高起在《阳

fountain, preserves the taste of morning. A new vessel, freshly made with purple clay, brings the tincture of spring" and this remains the earliest record of purple clay pot being a member of tea culture.

    In 1976, archaeologists excavated in Dingshu Town an ancient kiln dating back to the Song Dynasty (960-1279). With a length of about 10 meters and a width of 1 meter, the kiln was filled with fragments or broken parts of early purple clay products. In addition, two purple clay vessels were unearthed in a dilapidated mine dated back to the Southern Song Dynasty (1127-1279). These two important discoveries provide strong evidence that purple clay pot first appeared in the Northern Song Dynasty (960-1127), and the shapes of

• 北宋褐釉茶碗
Brown Glazed Tea Bowl (Northern Song Dynasty, 960-1127)

• 宋代紫砂壶
Purple Clay Teapot (Song Dynasty, 960-1279)

羡茗壶系》中称他为"紫砂壶的创始人"。

金沙寺位于宜兴东南20公里处，相传明弘治正德年间，寺内有一老僧名智静，今人称其为"金沙寺僧"。金沙寺僧常与周围缸瓮业主及陶工来往，因此谙熟制陶技艺。由于当时饮茶习惯正向壶泡

vessels indicate the earliest purple clay pot was used to brew tea, which was very consistent with the custom of "Tea Contest" popular at that time. However, purple clay vessels were simply new things in the Song Dynasty, and they were different from current purple clay pot in terms of form and popularity.

During the Ming Dynasty (1368-1644) when a monk from Jinsha Temple changed the situation. The monk — a milestone figure in Yixing teapot history, was said to have been the founder of purple clay pot according to Zhou Gaoqi, a famed tea connoisseur, in his *Yangxian Minghu Xi* (*A Collection of Yangxian Teapot Masterworks*).

Jinsha Temple is located 20 kilometers to the southeast of Yixing. Legend has it that during the Zhengde period of the Ming Dynasty (1488-1521) there lived in this temple an old monk with Buddhist name "Zhijing", who was known to the secular world as the "Jinsha Monk". He was used to exchange ideas with pottery shop owners and potters in his neighborhood, so he was familiar with pottery making. At the time, teapot steeping gradually became the main trend of tea drinking. Inspired, the monk refined the clay into fine powder and

方式转变，金沙寺僧于是澄练细土，制作紫砂器，供人泡茶。据传金沙寺僧喜用紫砂泥制作容量颇大的圆形壶，既不留款，也不钤印，仅以指纹为标志。由于其作品并不署款，所以难以认定是否有作品流传于世。金沙寺僧的制壶技艺很高，在当时已负盛名，后来被人尊为紫砂壶的始祖。

made purple clay wares for tea drinkers. It is said that the monk loved to make large round teapots, leaving neither inscriptions nor seals on them except his fingerprint as a symbol. Because of this, it is difficult to identify whether or not his works survived till today. Renowned at the time for his superior skills in making teapots, he was later considered as the founder of purple clay pot.

"始陶异僧"的传说

关于紫砂泥的发现，有一个颇具神话色彩的故事。在明代周高起所著的中国第一本记载宜兴紫砂壶的著作《阳羡茗壶系》中，记载了紫砂泥被发现的故事："相传壶土初出用时，先有异僧经行村落，自呼曰卖富贵土，人群嗤之。僧曰：'贵不要买，买富何如？'因引村叟，指山中产土之穴，去及发之，果备五色，灿若披锦。"从此以后，一传十，十传百，丁蜀地区山村的村民都来挖掘山间的"富贵土"，并开始烧造最早的紫砂陶器。这便是"始陶异僧"的传说。

A Legend of the Gorgeous Soil

There was a rather mythical story regarding the origin of purple clay, which was recorded in *Yangxian Minghu Xi*, a book about Yixing teapot by Zhou Gaoqi of the Ming Dynasty (1368-1644) in China, and the story starts like this: "According to the legend, there was once a monk who wanted to sell a kind of soil named *Fugui* (Rich & Noble) in a village. The villagers, however, all sniffed at him. The monk then said to the villagers if they did not want the "noble", they might choose the "rich", and he went on to lead the villagers somewhere in the mountains to excavate this kind of soil. When the soil was dug, everybody was amazed to find that it was gorgeous in color. Message spread, villagers across this region flocked to dig the *Fugui* Soil, and since then they have started firing the earliest purple clay ware."

- **《阳羡茗壶系》书影**

  《阳羡茗壶系》是已知的第一部关于紫砂壶的专著，作者为明代文人周高起。该书对紫砂工艺的发展脉络及制壶名家逐一叙述，并列其生年、风格特点及所见传器等，还论及泥品和品茗用壶的选择。

  Book Cover of *Yangxian Minghu Xi*

  Yangxian Minghu Xi is the earliest known monograph on purple clay pot, the author of which is Zhou Gaoqi—a scholar of the Ming Dynasty (1368-1644). This book describes the development process of purple clay techniques and introduces one by one the masters in pottery making, while provides their detailed information such as their years, style, characteristics, their masterworks, etc.; it also elaborates on the selection of clay and tips on using tea wares.

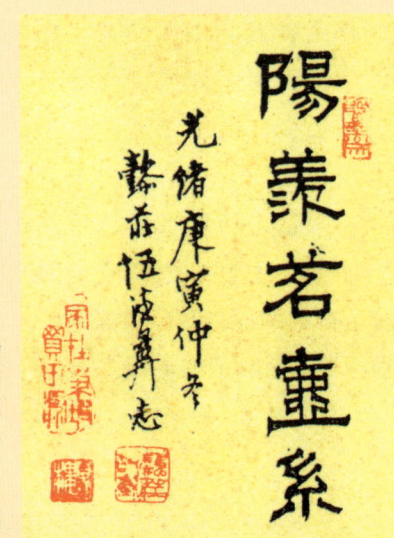

  ## 明代紫砂壶

  紫砂壶由金沙寺僧创制之后，就进入了蓬勃发展的时期，出现了许多杰出的艺人，如供春、时大彬等，从此紫砂壶艺正式走上历史舞台。明万历年间，紫砂壶三大壶式（花货、光货、筋囊货）已基本确立，并均有上佳作品问世，使紫砂壶积淀了更多的文化内涵和文人气息。这一时期是紫砂壶艺史上第一个鼎盛时期。

  明代的紫砂壶，造型较多吸取

  ## Pots of the Ming Dynasty

  From the Jinsha Monk onwards, purple clay pot entered into a period of vigorous development, purple clay artisans also came forth in a great number — Gong Chun, Shi Dabin, to name a few; this brought the art of purple clay pot into a new era. In the Wanli period, the three major styles of the purple clay pot, namely smooth pot, sculpture pot and veined pot, had basically taken shape, with each having its masterworks, adding

了铜锡器皿造型的特点，筋囊货造型较多。明式家具简洁凝重的风格对紫砂壶艺的影响也是随处可见。总体来说，明代紫砂壶造型浑厚，古朴大方，比例协调，泥质颗粒较粗。

more cultural connotation and scholarly note to purple clay pottery. This is the first flourishing period of the purple clay pot.

Purple clay pots of the Ming Dynasty (1368-1644) borrowed many elements and characteristics from copper and tin wares. As a result, veined pieces were prevalent in this period. The art of purple clay pot also owed much to the simple and dignified styles of Ming-era furniture. In general, teapots are characterized by their vigorous shape, plain and elegant note, harmonious scale and coarse clay grains.

- 紫砂海棠式提梁大壶（明）
Big Purple Clay Pot with Upper Handle in Begonia Shape (Ming Dynasty, 1368-1644)

- 紫砂雕漆提梁壶（明）
Carved Lacquer Purple Clay Pot with Upper Handle (Ming Dynasty, 1368-1644)

- 泥绘壶（明）
Clay Painting Teapot (Ming Dynasty, 1368-1644)

清代紫砂壶

清代的紫砂壶艺进一步繁荣，尤其是康熙、雍正、乾隆三朝，社会稳定，经济繁荣，紫砂壶品种日益增多，除大量生产壶、杯等茶具外，还生产有花盆、玩具、雅玩陈设等。紫砂壶的形制多姿多彩，出现了仿古形、花果形、几何形等壶式；泥料配色也更丰富，朱泥、紫色泥仍为主体，还有白泥、乌泥、黄泥、梨皮泥、松花泥等多种泥色；制壶技艺和装饰手法也都有新的创造和发明。

这一时期，紫砂壶制作工艺精湛，备受皇室青睐，因此成为贡品，开始进入宫廷。泥绘、描金、彩釉、炉均、堆贴、篆印等装饰手法也应运而

Pots of the Qing Dynasty

The prosperity of purple clay pots was further enhanced in the Qing Dynasty (1616-1911), especially in the period of emperors Kangxi, Yongzheng and Qianlong. In such an age of social stability and economic thriving, teapot varieties saw a rapid increase. In addition to the mass production of pots, cups and other tea sets, purple clay products also extended to flower pots, toys, elegant playthings, furnishings and so on. In this period, the shapes of purple clay pots were varied, including archaized shape, fruit shape, geometric shape and other shapes; the varieties of clay colors were also richer than ever. Aside from *Zhuni* (cinnabar clay) and purple clay still as the main hue, the clays came in more colors — white, black, yellow, pear-skin and *Songhua* (a color

- 乾隆御题诗烹茶图阔底壶（清）
  Wide Bottom Teapot with Qianlong's Inscriptions and a Picture of Making Tea (Qing Dynasty, 1616-1911)

百果壶（清）
Tea Pot with Fruit Decoration (Qing Dynasty, 1616-1911)

龙首三足壶（清）
Three-legged Teapot with Spout in Shape of Loong Head (Qing Dynasty, 1616-1911)

生。北京故宫博物院就藏有乾隆御制诗紫砂壶、紫砂茶叶罐等，以及一套乾隆外出时携带的紫砂茶具。

嘉庆、道光年间，紫砂壶的形制和装饰发生了巨大的改变，这种改变是由于文人参与紫砂壶的设计而引起的。文人参与紫砂壶艺虽前朝已有，但这一时期更加盛行，甚至成为紫砂壶艺的主流。制壶艺

that resembles the surface of preserved egg), while pottery skills and decorative techniques benefited from new creations and inventions as well.

Furthermore, with superior skills, purple clay pots of this period were favored by the royal family so much that they became a tribute. This also gave rise to the emergence of decorative techniques as clay painting, gold tracing, colored glaze, *Lujun*, tessellation, printing, pasting, etc. The Palace Museum houses several purple clay wares, among which the teapot and the tea canister with Emperor Qianlong's inscriptions, along with a tea set that the emperor carried during his trip, are typical examples.

In the Jiaqing and Daoguang periods, both the shapes and decorations of purple clay pots underwent dramatic changes, resulting from the involvement in its design of literati, who had long been concerned with this and made it a prevalent trend in this period. Teapots of this time mostly emphasized inscription-oriented decorative ways — calligraphy, painting and seal were common approaches, the style of thin and compact beauty dominant in the early Qing Dynasty was replaced with elegant simplicity. Smooth pots, decorated with terse lines on the pot

人们大都摒弃了清初注重妍巧的风气，式样转趋典雅古朴，以书法、绘画、篆刻为主的刻画装饰成为最主要的装饰手段。紫砂壶的壶式以光货为主，壶体上的装饰线条也较为简练，以突出表现文人所喜欢的书法、绘画、篆刻等内容。这些变化，使紫砂壶的书卷气、金石味更加浓烈。

清代出现了许多紫砂大师，如陈鸣远、邵大亨、黄玉麟、邵大赦、何心舟、王东石、蒋德林、吴阿根、蒋万丰等。

body, became mainstream. This was convenient for preferences of the literati class — calligraphic works, painting and seal carving — to be exhibited, which added a strong scholarly and epigraphic note to the teapot.

A great deal of purple clay masters emerged in the Qing Dynasty (1616-1911), including Chen Mingyuan, Shao Daheng, Huang Yulin, Shao Dashe, He Xinzhou, Wang Dongshi, Jiang Delin, Wu Agen, Jiang Wanfeng, and others.

来自宫廷的垂青

中国的很多帝王都有饮茶的习俗，有的嗜茶如命，有的好取茶名，有的则专为茶叶著书立说，甚至还有给进贡名茶之人封官加爵的。如宋徽宗赵佶，工于书画，通晓百艺，尤其对茶叶的评品颇有见地，著有《大观茶论》一书。由于赵佶的大力提倡，出现了"茶盛于宋"的景象。

清代的乾隆皇帝也酷爱饮茶，民间流传了许多关于他与茶的传说。从乾隆年间开始，宜兴紫砂壶作为正式贡品进献朝廷。这种来自宫廷的垂青对宜兴紫砂壶制作工艺的发展有着很大的影

- **宜兴窑紫砂描金瓜棱壶（清）**
  Melon-shaped Teapot with Gold Tracing From Yixing Kiln (Qing Dynasty, 1616-1911)

响，比如紫砂壶在清代开始加彩上釉，就是为了满足皇室的需求。

宜兴有不少工匠曾为宫廷制作加彩的贡品茗壶，北京故宫博物院所藏清内务府造办处档案就有这样的记载："乾隆二十三年十月五日，苏州织造……送到……宜兴壶四件。"

The Imperial Court's Favorite

Many of the Chinese emperors were fond of tea — some crazy about it, some loving to bename it, while some writing books on it, and some going so far as to grant high official posts to those who offer top quality tea as tribute. Zhao Ji, the versatile Emperor of the Northern Song Dynasty (960-1127) was a typical example. Accomplished in painting, calligraphy and connoisseur appreciation of tea leaves, he was the author of *Da Guancha Lun* (A Concise Encyclopedia of Tea in the Northern Song Dynasty), and it was his conscious advocacy that made a zenith of tea culture in his day.

The Emperor Qianlong of the Qing Dynasty (1616-1911) was not an exception. Legends of his passion for tea abounds outside the imperial court. Yixing purple clay pot, since his reign, has been admirably favored by the Qing Court and eventually became an official tribute. This made a great impact on the techniques of Yixing pottery, for example, the coloring and glazing of the teapot owed much to what the royal family wanted of the purple clay works.

In Yixing, a group of artisans had made colored teapots as tributes for the imperial court, as was recorded in a document housed in the Palace Museum, "On the 5th of the tenth lunar month, 1759, four Yixing teapots were presented by Suzhou local government to the imperial court … "

- 《清明茶宴图》（唐）
  A Tea Banquet at Qingming (Tang Dynasty, 618-907)

民国紫砂壶

民国时期，紫砂壶产业的命运颇具波折。清末至民国初期，紫砂陶业仍缓慢地发展着。一批商家在上海、宜兴、无锡、天津、杭州等地开设专门店，从宜兴定制紫砂壶，并聘用名艺人制作，使宜兴紫砂壶不仅销往国内各大城市，还远销日本、东南亚，以及欧美等地区。

这一时期紫砂壶的壶式大多沿袭清代，少有创新，偏重刻画装饰。刻画纹饰以摹刻名画、不同书体的书法、碑版、青铜器铭文、砖瓦古陶文等为主。一大批紫砂艺人涌现出来，如程寿珍、俞国良、范大生、李宝珍、汪宝根等。他们技艺精妙，擅于仿古，创作了许多佳作。

• 松鼠葡萄壶（民国）
Teapot with Patterns of Squirrel and Grapes (Minguo Period, 1912-1949)

Pots of the Minguo Period (1912-1949)

During the Minguo period, the purple clay industry experienced a setback. However, from the late Qing Dynasty to the early Minguo period, it was still in a slow development when a group of business opened exclusive pottery shops in Shanghai, Yixing, Wuxi, Tianjin and Hangzhou, and commissioned teapots from famed artisans of Yixing, so that these tea wares were not only sold to major cities across the country but also exported to Japan, Southeast Asia, and the West.

Mainly in imitation of the Qing Dynasty (1616-1911) and with less innovation, teapot shapes of this period laid stress on carving decorations — paintings, calligraphic works in various scripts, stone, bronze and tile inscriptions were exquisitely executed on tea wares. Meanwhile, famous craftsmen came forth in great numbers — Cheng Shouzhen, Yu Guoliang, Fan Dasheng, Li Baozhen, Wang Baogen, to name a few. With superior skills and excelled in following the ancient styles, they brought many masterworks, some of which won prizes in international expositions.

- 竹段壶（民国）
  Teapot in Shape of Bamboo Stem (Minguo Period, 1912-1949)

- 瓜型壶（民国）
  Melon-shaped Teapot (Minguo Period, 1912-1949)

有的还在国际博览会上获了奖。

抗日战争爆发后，宜兴乃至整个中国的紫砂陶业都陷入了低谷，许多紫砂大师在贫病交困中死去，从业人员只剩下二十余人，几尽人亡艺绝的境地。

During the war of resistance against Japanese agression, however, the pottery industry of Yixing and the whole country was caught in a trough, many purple clay masters died in poverty and only a few survived, both the industry and craftspeople were left destroyed.

店号壶

店号壶是指一些著名紫砂壶店铺出品的紫砂壶，所用的泥料、烧制方法和工艺手法都非常有特色。店号壶起源于清末，当时宜兴的制陶业呈现较为繁荣的局面，经营紫砂壶生意的商人便纷纷在江苏、山东、安徽等地的城市开设专门经营紫砂壶的门店。他们向宜兴的紫砂艺人们订制大量紫砂壶，并加盖自己的店号名称，表示是自家店号的产品。当时较为著名的店号有吴德盛陶器行、铁画轩陶器公司、陈鼎和陶器店等。店号壶一般都是大批量生产，其中也不乏有名手制作的。由于它们价格低，实用性强，因此很受人们欢迎。

Shop Mark Teapot

Shop Mark Teapot refers to those produced by famous pottery shops. Clay materials, firing methods and techniques applied in this kind of teapot were often of distinctive characteristics. Shop Mark Teapot originated in the late Qing Dynasty; at that time pottery industry was thriving in Yixing, and businessmen dealing with purple clay products flooded to open pottery shops in Jiangsu, Shandong, Anhui and other places, to sell teapots they ordered from Yixing craftsmen. On each pot was carved the name of the shop as the brand identification. Famous shops of this time included Wu Desheng, the Pottery Corporation of *Tiehua Xuan*, Chen Dinghe Pottery Factory and so on. Generally, these teapots were manufactured in high volume, of which some were made by famed artisans. Because of their affordability and practicability, they were very popular among people.

- 民国时期的著名店号款
  Shop Mark in Seal Carving Form (Minguo Period, 1912-1949)

当代紫砂壶

中华人民共和国成立后，紫砂陶业得到恢复和发展。流散各地的紫砂艺人们被政府组织起来，回到宜兴，重新制造紫砂壶，紫砂艺人队伍逐渐壮大。

20世纪70年代，紫砂壶的生产出现了新的艺术高峰，涌现出众多

Pots of Modern Day

After the founding of the People's Republic of China in 1949, purple clay industry was revived and experienced growth once again. Many of the artisans, scattered to the winds, were found and summoned by the government. They revitalized the pottery industry of Yixing. The number of purple clay artisans,

紫砂大师，人们对紫砂壶的兴趣进一步升温，在港台地区、东南亚地区都出现了紫砂收藏热。

20世纪80年代起，众多紫砂艺人融合西方的艺术观念，开拓了紫砂艺术的新天地。一批具有较高文

in this favorable situation, gradually increased as well.

In 1970s, with a great number of masters emerging, the purple clay industry ushered in a new era. People's interest in purple clay pots has further increased, and there has been a collection

- 当代紫砂壶
  Pot of Modern Times

当代紫砂壶
Pot of Modern Times

化水平和艺术造诣的艺术家，在绘画、文学、金石学家们的支持和参与下，推陈出新，创作出一大批当代紫砂陶器，使紫砂行业呈现出前所未有的繁荣局面。

国内著名的艺术院校如中央工艺美术学院、景德镇陶瓷学院（今景德镇陶瓷大学）、南京艺术学院，以及其他的艺术院校，相继开办了短期的培训班、进修班，使改

craze in China's Hong Kong and Taiwan, and regions of Southeast Asia.

Since the 1980s, many artisans have combined the artistic concept of art of the West, and opened up a new world for teapot art. In the meantime, a group of artisans, featuring high levels of literacy and artistic skills, innovatively created a large number of contemporary purple clay wares with the help and support of painters, litterati and epigraphists, bringing unprecedented prosperity to the

革开放后涌入国门的当代艺术思潮和设计思想得以传播，也让紫砂陶业得到了空前的发展。

当代紫砂陶艺更注重个性创作，器形上与传统紫砂制品截然不同。传统紫砂壶工艺具有一个显著的特点，就是仿制，甚至出现过"千人仿一壶"的现象。一个新壶式一旦出了名，业内人士就会纷纷仿制。先是形似，然后神似，最后再有所突破，形成自己的风格。许多紫砂艺人一生都在仿制，即便是有所创新，也仅仅是在壶嘴、壶盖、壶把上稍作调整。而当代紫砂陶艺则摒弃了这一思想，强调个性的张扬，强调有感而发，使紫砂陶业呈现出别样的繁荣景象。

purple clay industry.

Also, the Central Academy of Fine Arts, Jingdezhen Ceramic Institute (now Jingdezhen Ceramic University), Nanjing Institute of the Arts, among other domestic art institutions have held short-term training and refresher courses, enabling contemporary art concepts and design ideas brought by the Reform and Opening Up to spread, and bringing another period of unprecedented development for purple clay industry.

Modern teapots, however, lay more emphasis on individuality. Their shapes are totally different from traditional pieces, the obvious feature of which is imitation. It is said that a popular traditional style would have been followed by a crowd of artisans, starting from exact copy and then to spiritual likeness, finally forming an innovative style of one's own. For many purple clay artisans, imitation spanned their entire life. In their works few creative ideas had been executed other than minor adjustments on the spout, the lid and the handle; while their modern counterparts, ridding of this concept, stress individuality and emotional expression, elevating the purple clay art to a new level.

> 紫砂壶与中国茶

中国的茶文化源远流长，古人从"食茶"发展到"饮茶"，再到"品茶"的过程中，逐渐形成了关于茶叶、茶具、用水、烹煮、饮用的独到见解，赋予了饮茶这一活动深厚的文化内涵。也正是在这个过程中，紫砂壶应运而生，它的历史虽不久远，但却后来居上，成为"茶具之首"。茶坛有了它，茶的清香从此便不再断绝，甚至尤胜从前。

饮茶与茶具的流变

明代的许次纾在《茶疏》中说："茶滋于水，水藉于器，汤成于火，四者相负，缺一则废。"这强调了茶、水、器、火四者之间的密切关系。因此，要深入地了解紫砂壶，就不能不说到中国的茶文

> Purple Clay Pot and Chinese Tea

Chinese tea culture enjoys a long history. In the evolvement of ancient tea practices — from eating to drinking to enjoying — a general concept gradually formed, containing tea leaves, tea wares, service of water, brewing and drinking method, and tea drinking, was thereby given a profound cultural connotation. This process was echoed by the purple clay pot. Although it was only a rising star, it outshined all other tea wares, and the fragrance of tea, thanks to its birth, was better than ever.

The Evolution of Tea Drinking and Tea Sets

Xu Cishu, a tea connoisseur of the Ming Dynasty (1368-1644) and author of *From Picking to Drinking — A Complete Guide to Chinese Tea*, emphasized the

《撵茶图》（南宋 刘松年）
The Painting of Tea Grinding, by Liu Songnian (Southern Song Dynasty, 1127-1279)

化，尤其是茶具的演变历史。

早在西周初年，茶就在古人的生活中开始普及。此时的用茶方式主要是烹煮，所用的"茶具"与餐具、酒具等是通用的，一般为青铜质的鼎或陶质的钵。

close ties between tea, water, ware and fire in this monograph :" Tea moistens in the water, while water relies on tea ware, and fire determines the tea soup, these four factors are interrelated, none of them is not indispensable." To achieve an in-depth understanding of the purple clay pot, Chinese tea culture especially the evolvement of tea wares are not to be ignored.

彩绘陶鐎壶（西汉）
Painted Ceramic Teapot (Western Han Dynasty, 206B.C.-25A.D.)

• 鎏金银茶罗（唐）
Silver-gilt Tea Container (Tang Dynasty, 618-907)

秦汉时期，茶越来越被人们所重视，为了方便运输和贮存，人们将茶叶制成饼，烘干保存。这一时期，茶具从餐饮器皿中独立出来，专门为饮茶而用。东汉时期，陶瓷茶具逐渐兴起，茶具的种类更加丰富。

到了隋唐时期，饮茶已成为人们日常生活中必不可少的一部分，社会上嗜茶成风，煎茶法十分流行。中国的茶叶种植面积大增，产量大幅度提高，茶店、茶铺渐多，茶具进一步发展。

宋代，茶业愈加繁荣，上至皇室、贵族，下至平民百姓，皆盛行饮茶。宋人的饮茶方式非常优雅，也十分讲究，这与宋代对文化的重视有密切关系。宋代文人的地位相

As far back as the early Western Zhou Dynasty (1046B.C.-771B.C.) when tea began to spread, cooking tea was the common practice in this period. Tea, wine and dine shared the same vessels, of bronze tripod ware or ceramic bowls in general.

During the Qin (221B.C.-207B.C.) and Han (206B.C.- 220A.D.) dynasties, tea gained more attention. In order to facilitate transport and storage, tea was made into tea cakes, then dried up for preservation. In this period, tea wares were separated from dining vessels to be specifically used for tea drinking. In the Eastern Han Dynasty (25-220), with the gradual rise of ceramic tea wares, the type of tea vessels grew more abundant.

In the Sui (581-618) and Tang (618-907) dynasties, tea drinking was a great fashion among people, while tea cooking became a popular practice. This gave rise to a significant increase in China's tea acreage and yield. Meanwhile, tea shops and tea houses were opened one after another, promoting the further development of tea wares.

The tea industry experienced an unprecedented prosperity in the Song Dynasty (960-1279) when tea drinking was a ubiquitous practice among the

对较高，饮茶自然更加追求雅趣品味，最具特色的品饮方式就是点茶和斗茶。这一时期，茶具的组成有了明显变化，基本固定为茶碗和茶壶。当时制作茶具的主要材料为瓷。

　　明清两代，散茶开始流行，也就是人们今天所饮用的茶叶。用茶的方式也以泡饮为主，茶具也简化为壶、杯，但其制作工艺却是越来越精致，对品质的要求也越来越高。也正是在这一时期，紫砂壶以其优越的宜茶性及高妙的制作工艺，在各种材质的茶具中逐渐脱颖而出，成为宫廷和民间皆喜爱的茶具。

royal family, the gentry class and civilians. The upper class of Song era, stressing art and culture, brought up the elegant and meticulous way of tea drinking. Furthermore, literati drank tea and pursued more elegant taste. Tea dripping and tea contest, then the most characteristic drinking methods, were good examples. During this period, significant changes have taken place in the system of tea wares. Tea bowl and teapot were the basic members, and they were chiefly made of porcelain.

　　In the Ming (1368-1644) and Qing (1616-1911) dynasties, loose tea — present-day tea leaves — began its rise to popularity, and tea steeping became a major practice, tea wares were thus simplified to pots and cups but were made with finer craftsmanship and higher quality requirements. It was in this period that purple clay pot stood out in tea wares of various varieties, and was consequently much sought after by the imperial court and civilians.

● 紫砂加彩大茶叶罐（清）
Colored Large Purple Clay Tea Jar (Qing Dynasty, 1616-1911)

古人的饮茶方式

　　古人的用茶方式与今人有很大不同。唐代以前,古人用茶的方法属于粗放式的煮茶法,即把它当成食物来烹煮,甚至加有葱姜等调味料。唐代,煎茶法流行,且程序极为复杂,对煎水、备茶等每一个步骤都极为重视,不再加入精盐调味,成为完全的清饮,保留了茶叶固有的清香。煎茶法将饮茶活动提升到了精神境界和艺术创造的高度,极大地推动了中国茶文化的发展和茶具的演变。

　　宋代流行点茶法,不再将茶直接放入容器中烹煮,而是先将饼茶碾碎,放在杯或碗中,用容器烧水至沸腾,先注入少量沸水将碎茶调成糊状,然后再注入沸水冲点。点茶法与今天主流的泡饮茶的方法比较相似,相对于煎茶法来说更为"先进",因此很快被人们所接受。

　　到了明代,人们的饮茶方式又发生了改变。农民出身的开国皇帝朱元璋认为点茶法过于繁琐,下令摒弃饼茶,而采用一泡即喝的简便方法,这便是今天的饮茶。虽然当时人们饮茶的方式简便了,但对茶和水的品质却有了更高的要求,讲究在清雅的诗境中品茗,对泡茶、观茶色、烫壶等都非常讲究,开始钟爱不吸茶香、不损茶色的紫砂茶具。

- 《竹林品茗图》(清 任伯年)
  Enjoying Tea in a Bamboo Grove, by Ren Bonian
  (Qing Dynasty, 1616-1911)

Ancient Ways of Tea Drinking

Ancient and modern people differ greatly in tea drinking practices. Prior to the Tang Dynasty when unconstrained ways were dominant, tea was cooked like food with even ginger, green onion and other seasonings added. In the Tang Dynasty (618-907), people were popular with sencha. It is a practice with an extremely complicated process, in which each step including water boiling, tea preparation, etc., were given great attention to. In this process involving only tea leaves and water, salt was no longer a necessary additive so as to retain the natural fragrance of tea. Sencha elevated Chinese tea drinking to a spiritual area and level of artistic creation, greatly promoting the development of Chinese tea culture and the evolution of tea wares.

In the Song Dynasty (960-1279), tea dripping became a very popular custom. Instead of cooking the cake tea directly in a container, people put pulverized tea powder into bowls. By mixing with a little boiling water, they stirred the mixture to paste, then poured boiling water again. Tea dripping had something in common with the present-day tea infusion, and it was quickly accepted by drinkers because of its convenience.

In the Ming Dynasty (1368-1644), tea drinking practice experienced another change. Zhu Yuanzhang, the founding emperor with a peasant background, who was sick of the cumbersome tea dripping, ordered to abandon it, and promoted a simple way of single infusion, which was almost the way of today's tea steeping. While the way of tea drinking was simpler at the time, it put forward higher requirements for tea and water, emphasizing tea drinking atmosphere, tea steeping, appreciation of tea soup color as well as warming up of teapot. In line with these, purple clay tea wares, capable of retaining the fragrance and color of tea, became everybody's favorites.

• 煎茶
Sencha

斗茶

斗茶是中国古代文人雅士的一种"雅玩"。斗茶是评比新茶品序的一项比赛活动,比技巧、斗输赢,富有趣味性。斗茶的胜负取决于汤色和汤花。汤色即茶水的颜色,标准是以纯白为上,青白、灰白、黄白,则等而下之。汤花即指汤面泛起的泡沫。汤花的色泽也是以鲜白为上;其水痕出现晚者为胜,早者为负。在斗茶中,紫砂壶发挥着重要的作用,这不仅是因为紫砂器具有很好的宜茶性,还因为紫砂器便于观察茶色,便于显现白色茶沫,因而成为斗茶者的首选。

Tea Contest

Tea contest is a kind of elegant and interesting activity favored by ancient Chinese literati and scholars. It is used to assess the new tea of each year involving servicing techniques and tea quality. In this contest, color and foam of tea soup are decisive factors. For the color, pure white is deemed the finest, superior over greenish, greyish and yellowish white. Foam refers to a thin layer of spray formed on the surface of tea soup. Again, pure white foam is considered the top one, and the water trace, determined by the time of occurrence, is also a criterion. The later it appears, the higher position it will get. Purple clay pot plays an important role in this process not only because it fits in well with tea but also provides convenience in observing the color of tea soup and displaying the white tea foam, thus becoming the first choice for tea contestants.

• 《斗茶图》(明 顾炳)
Tea Contest by Gu Bing (Ming Dynasty, 1368-1644)

紫砂壶的宜茶性

紫砂壶具有良好的宜茶性，"茗注莫妙于砂，壶之精者又莫过于阳羡"，这是明末清初的文学家李渔对紫砂壶的评价。紫砂壶透气性好、保温性好，宜于茶性发挥，同时经久耐磨。泡出的茶，汤、色、味、气俱佳，其砂质含有较多微量元素，非常宜于人体吸收。具体来说，紫砂壶的宜茶性主要表现在以下几个方面：

（1）用紫砂壶泡茶能保持茶的原味，使茶水的色、香、味俱佳，且香味持久不散。

（2）用紫砂壶冲泡的茶，放得时间再长也不会馊，甚至在暑天隔

• 紫砂茶具组合
Purple Clay Tea Set

The Suitability of Purple Clay Pot for Tea

The purple clay pot is a good company for tea. Li Yu, a litterateur of the late Ming and early Qing dynasties, spoke of it in this way "No material is better than clay in making teapots, and no teapot is better than the one from Yangxian". The purple clay pot is durable and enjoys good permeability and heat preservation, which is able to bring the best flavor out of tea. Tea steeped in clay pot has excellent soup, color and fragrance, while the high content of trace elements contained in the clay can be easily absorbed by the human body. Specifically, the advantages of purple clay pots are mainly in the following areas:

1. It can keep the original fragrance, taste and color of tea, retaining the aroma of tea for a long time.

2. The tea in the purple clay pot can remain fresh after being left for a lengthy period, producing no dirty traces even in summer. This eases the rinse of the pot.

3. After prolonged use, the inner wall of a teapot will develop a special coating — the teapot can absorb a tiny amount of tea during brewing — the boiling water alone will bring out the fragrance of tea.

夜也不起腻苔，方便洗涤及保持茶壶自身的清洁。

（3）长期使用的紫砂壶，壶内壁会积聚"茶锈"，即使不放茶叶，注入沸水也会有茶香味。

（4）紫砂壶耐热性和透气性良好，可以承受冷热的急剧变化，比如在冬天往壶内注入沸水，壶体不会炸裂；同时紫砂传热缓慢，泡茶后握壶不会烫手。

（5）紫砂壶经过长久使用，器身会因抚摸擦拭，变得更加光润。

当然，并不是所有茶叶都宜用紫砂壶来冲泡，不同的茶系需要选择不同的壶。一般来说，紫砂壶用来泡半发酵茶或全发酵茶最好，比如铁观音、乌龙、普洱等。而龙井、毛峰等绿茶则不宜用紫砂壶冲泡，因为紫砂壶的保温性很强，长时间保持高温会破坏绿茶中的维生素。

4. Purple clay pot is characterized by ideal heat resistance and air permeability that enable it to withstand rapid changes in temperatures. For example, the pot will not crack in cold weather when pouring boiling water in it, and similarly it will not scald one's hands while holding boiling water thanks to the feature of slow heat transfer.

5. With age, the body of the teapot will become smoother owing to frequent caressing and wiping.

Of course, purple clay would not be appropriate for all kinds of tea. It is suggested that different teapots be used for each style of tea. Normally, it best suits fermented or semi-fermented tea including *Tieguanyin*, Oolong, Pu-erh, etc. However, *Longjing*, *Maofeng*, among other green tea, are not to be steeped in it due to the thermal preservation feature. Prolonged high temperatures will destroy the vitamins in green tea.

紫砂茶艺
Tea Ceremony

闲暇的时候，捧上一把心仪的紫砂壶，品上一口醇香馥郁的茗茶，这是许多爱茶人追求的生活。茶可独饮，以美心修德；也可邀上几位知己，通过沏茶、赏茶、闻茶、饮茶，增进友谊。

可以说，紫砂壶与茶是天生的搭档。以下便将简单的紫砂茶艺展示出来：

Drinking aromatic tea while appreciating a favorite teapot at leisure, is an ideal quality of life that many tea enthusiasts long for. Tea drinking can be practiced alone, to enhance moral and cultural cultivation, or shared with a couple of friends, to promote friendship in a pleasant atmosphere of steeping, enjoying, smelling and drinking.

In conclusion, purple clay pot and tea are partners in nature, and here we will introduce you the relevant tea ceremony.

- 温壶
  Warming Up of Teapot

- 投茶
  Tea Application

- 泡茶
  Tea Steeping

- 润茶
  Tea Moistening

• 分茶
Tea Soup Allocation

• 敬茶
Presenting Tea

• 品茶
Tea Tasting

温壶、温茶与温杯

不同的地区，茶艺、茶俗不尽相同。在南方，人们习惯在饮茶前先"温壶""温茶""温杯"，即对茶壶、茶叶、茶杯进行"提温"，以获得更好的口感。

"温壶"是指在放茶叶之前，先用热水把茶壶温热，目的是在正式泡茶时，防止冰冷的茶壶吸收水的热量而降低水温，达不到泡出茶香的效果。具体做法是：将水加热至稍高于泡茶用水温度，然后提起水壶，以10—15厘米的高度，以绕倒的方式将壶冲至八分满。最后盖上壶盖，焖盖大约1分钟。

"温茶"即在泡茶之前，将茶叶先加热一下。"温茶"具有两个作用，一是提高茶叶的温度，避免它吸收水的热量，使泡茶的水温更接近所需要的温度；二是能够更好地把茶叶泡开，同时也能够初步鉴别茶叶品质的优劣。具体方法有两种：一是将壶温热后，把适量的茶叶投进去，然后盖上壶盖，仅利用壶内的热度对茶叶进行加热，焖盖约1分钟后，嗅闻茶叶的香气，即所谓"汤前香"。二是将壶温热后，把茶叶投进去，然后冲入开水，冲水方法为绕倒。水将茶叶打湿后即盖上壶盖，并马上将水倒出。这样一来，茶叶也能够吸收热量与水分，达到温茶的目的。

"温杯"即指为茶杯提温，方法是将热水冲进杯中稍待片刻再倒出即可。"温杯"有两个作用，一是将杯子烫热，免得茶汤倒进后热量被吸收，导致茶汤短时间就变冷，失去茶香；另一个作用就是让人端起杯子品茶时，手与嘴唇能感受到较舒适的温度。

Warming Up of Teapot, Tea and Teacup

Tea ceremonies and custom vary in different regions. In Southern China, people like to warm up the teapot, teacup and tea, to raise their temperature so as to achieve better taste.

Warming up of the teapot is to heat it with hot water before tea leaves are added. This aims to, prior to the formal steeping, prevent the absorption of heat by the cold teapot that consequently reduces the water temperature and that ultimately poses a negative impact on tea infusion. Specifically, the water is heated to a temperature slightly higher than what tea steeping needs, then to lift the kettle to a height of 10-15 centimeters over the teapot, to pour the water into the pot in a circular motion, with 80% of its capacity filled. Finally put the lid on, and simmer for about one minute.

Warming up of tea refers to the process of heating the tea leaves before steeping. This procedure has two roles: first to raise the temperature of tea leaves to keep the water temperature closer to the desired level; second, to better infuse tea leaves, and to initially identify the pros and cons of tea quality. There are two specific ways. One is to warm up the teapot, put the right amount of tea leaves into the pot, and then cover it with a lid, using only the heat of the teapot to warm the tea leaves, after simmering about one minute, sniff the aroma of tea, which is the so-called "fragrance before the tea soup". The other way: put the tea leaves into the warmed-up teapot, and then pour in boiling water in an around way, get the lid on when tea leaves are wet, and immediately pour out the water. In this

- 温壶
Warming Up of Teapot

way, tea leaves can also absorb heat and water, so as to achieve the purpose.

Warming up of teacups refers to the process of boosting the temperature of teacups, that is, pour hot water in the cup, wait a few moments and then pour the water out. This step works in two ways, too; one is to prevent the absorption of heat by cold teacups — which will result in a quick cooling down of tea soup and the subsequent loss of tea fragrance — when pouring in the tea soup; the other one is to allow the hands and lips feel more comfortable with the teacup.

以茶养壶

紫砂壶有一个非常特别的性能，就是需要"养"。一把紫砂壶烧成后，由于胎骨火气重，紫砂间微孔结构松，壶性很脆，容易受热胀冷缩的影响，只有经过"养"才能改变其"性格"，并能形成紫砂壶表面的包浆，愈用愈光亮，甚显高雅品位，增强紫砂壶"蕴味育香"的功能。

用过紫砂壶的人自然会发现，黑色紫砂壶在久养之后会呈瓦蓝黑色，黑而不墨，泽润生光；朱泥壶在久养之后会红若相思豆；刻有书画装饰的旧壶或古壶在久养之后，纹样的立体感会得到加强，更具书卷之气。

紫砂壶具有特殊的双气孔结

Nursing Teapot with Tea

Nursing is a particular practice for purple clay pot. A freshly fired teapot is susceptible to the impact of thermal expansion and contraction due to the brittleness caused by the loose pore-structure between clay particles. It is only through nursing that it can change the characteristic and form a special coating on its surface. With age, the teapot turns brighter and smoother, presenting an elegant taste and enhancing the feature of "retaining the flavor and cultivating the fragrance".

Inevitably, the user will find a fact that after prolonged nursing the black teapot presents a bluish-black color, delivering a blackish moistness and smoothness, while *Zhuni* or cinnabar clay will produce a color resembling that

• 用茶水养壶
Nursing Teapot with Tea Soup

构，能够很好地吸收茶汤茶味。因此，一把长期使用的紫砂壶，即使在不加茶叶的情况下，仅仅冲进沸水，也能"泡"出茶的香味来。鉴于紫砂壶的这种特性，在养壶时，一把紫砂壶最好坚持泡同一种茶，这样才能保持泡出的茶汤味道纯粹。

紫砂壶需要养，但如果养得不得当，壶的性能会大受损害。要让紫砂壶越用越好，还要有一套正确的养壶方法：

（1）使用紫砂壶之前和之后，要将壶身内外彻底清洗干净。无论是新壶还是旧壶，都要保持壶身内外的清洁卫生。

of jequirity; used or archaic teapot with decorative patterns on the body will have strengthened three-dimensional effect on its surface, to deliver a more scholarly note.

The dual-pore structure of purple clay enables the teapot to perfectly absorb the tea flavor. Therefore, a teapot, after a long-term use, is able to bring out the fragrance of tea by pouring in boiling water alone. In view of this feature, it would be better to partner a teapot with a certain kind of tea, in order to make the best flavor out of tea soup.

The method of nursing is also important. Inappropriate nursing will greatly damage the performance of a teapot. In this respect, proper ways are necessary to make the best of a teapot.

1. Before and after using the teapot, it should be cleaned thoroughly both inside and outside, regardless of old and new.

2. Keep away from oil stains. The dual-pore structure makes the teapot very sensitive to oil, and if contaminated, it must be cleaned immediately, otherwise the clay body will absorb the oil and leave traces, and will be unlikely to absorb tea fragrance as a result.

3. Nurse the teapot with tea rather

用湿布擦拭壶身
Wiping Pot Body with Wet Cloth

（2）切忌沾到油污。由于紫砂壶具有特殊的双气孔结构，因此最忌油污，如果不慎沾染上，必须马上清洗，否则土胎就会吸收并留下油痕，无法再吸收茶香。

（3）以茶养壶，不要以水养壶。用紫砂壶泡茶的次数越多，壶体吸收的茶汁就越多，当达到某种程度时，壶表面就会发出润泽如玉的光泽。

（4）在擦、刷紫砂壶时，力量要适度。清洗时，最好先使用软毛刷，将污渍轻轻刷洗后，再用开水冲净，然后用清洁的茶巾擦拭。

（5）紫砂壶使用完毕要彻底清洁并晾干，以免产生异味。

（6）虽然紫砂壶是越养越好，但也要适时地"休息"。频繁地用

than water. The more the teapot is used to steep, the more tea soup it will absorb. When reaching a certain level, the pot will gain a smooth luster like jade.

4. Wipe a purple clay pot with moderate force. It would be better to use a soft brush to scrub gently the stains before rinsing with boiling water. Finally use a clean towel to wipe the pot.

5. Lest produce unpleasant odor, the teapot is to be thoroughly cleaned and dried up after using.

6. While the teapot is getting better and better through nursing, it also needs "rest" after being frequently used for a period of time. This is to make its clay body dried up naturally and thoroughly, in order to better absorb tea soup in future use.

7. If idle for a long term, it should

过一段时间后，要让它"休息"一下，使其土胎自然彻底干燥，以便之后使用时更好地吸收茶汤。

（7）如果紫砂壶长期不用，应将其清洁之后放在通风处晾干，然后密闭储藏。重新使用前，应先用沸水冲烫一下。

按照上述这些养壶原则所"养"出来的紫砂壶，不但亮度能够经久不褪，而且也不怕人手触摸，可保持长期美观。

be cleaned and then placed in a well-ventilated place for drying up before being stored in an enclosure. It is suggested that it be rinsed with boiling water before reusing.

Following these principles, a teapot will be nursed to have not only durable brightness but a long-term beautiful appearance not afraid of touch by hands.

紫砂壶的手疗作用

用紫砂壶沏茶还具有手疗的作用。紫砂壶用沸水冲泡后，表面温度会达到50—80摄氏度，手接触后利于开张血管，达到舒经活血的作用。同时，紫砂壶表面有很多凹凸不平的沙砾，用手揉搓，具有养生的功效。

用紫砂壶手疗需掌握"五字诀"，即"揉、抚、捏、压、叩"。

"揉"：用力地摩擦茶壶的表面。置壶在茶桌上，一手覆在壶上，四指向下，大指向前。四指用力向内，在壶侧做上下运动。

"抚"：轻轻抚摸紫砂壶。用手掌笼盖壶上，整个手掌放在壶上或上下或左右轻磨壶身，从壶的一侧开始至壶盖，至壶身另一侧，至壶嘴、壶盖、壶子，周而复始，像抚摸婴儿一般。

"捏"：手指用力捏搓壶的菱或尖利的地方，然后边捏边旋转紫砂壶，称为"旋捏"，只捏不转称"停捏"，此法宜慢用力，使穴位酸胀为止。

"压"：将沏好茶水的紫砂壶置于一只手的手背上，另一只手扶住紫砂壶。并向下用力压，每分钟约30次。

"叩"：用指尖轻叩壶身，震荡指尖直到酸胀为止，切忌用指甲敲击紫砂壶，以免损伤紫砂壶。

Therapeutic Function of Purple Clay Pot

The therapeutic function of the purple clay pot is beneficial to one's hands. When holding boiling water, its surface temperature will reach 50-80 degrees Celsius, which helps open blood vessels and improve blood flow, while the uneven gravel on surface of the teapot, rubbed with hands, is good for one's health.

The therapeutic methods involve five practices: rubbing, stroking, pinching, pressing and knocking.

Rubbing means forcibly rubbing the surface of the teapot. Place the pot on the table, and put one hand on it, with four fingers downwards and the thumb forwards, force the four fingers tightly against the pot while moving them up and down.

Stroking is to stroke gently the teapot. Cover the pot with the palm of one's hand, rub the pot body softly, from top to bottom and left to right. To be specific, stroke the pot from bottom to up until reaching the lid, then go on stroking the other side of the body. Repeat the process as if caressing a baby.

Pinching refers to the process of holding forcibly the protruding parts of the teapot with fingers. The procedure of pinching the pot while rotating it is called *Xuannie*, and the one involving only pinching is *Tingnie*. Gradual and moderate force should be applied in this process whose purpose is to give the acupoint a sense of soreness and swellness.

The process of "Pressing" is as follows: place the teapot filled with hot tea on the back of one hand while the other hand holding onto it, and press it down firmly, about 30 times per minute.

Knocking is to softly knock at the pot body with fingertips. Repeat this action until soreness occurs in the fingertips. Do not use nails to knock at the teapot, so as not to damage it.

- 用紫砂壶进行手疗
Therapeutic Practice with Purple Clay Teapot

> 紫砂壶的文化内涵

紫砂壶不仅仅是一种艺术品，更具有深厚的文化内涵，具体体现在它的工艺、造型、以及各种装饰上。历代文人雅士和金石书画家们被紫砂壶所吸引，为紫砂壶赋予了高雅的气质和内涵，使之拥有了迷人的韵味和魅力。

文人名士与紫砂壶

紫砂壶艺能够日益精进，除了历代制壶艺人的贡献外，历代文人的参与功不可没，文人的参与使紫砂壶的形制更为雅致。

在古代，每当文人相聚，迎宾待客，必然烹茶品茗，吟诗作对，茶诗、茶词、茶画，佳作迭出。紫砂壶古朴淳厚、不媚不俗，与文人气质十分相近。文人玩壶，视为

> Cultural Connotations of Purple Clay Pot

The purple clay pot is not merely a work of art, and it is endowed with profound cultural connotation, which is reflected in its craftsmanship, shape and decorations. Literati, scholars, epigraphists as well as calligraphers and painters of past dynasties were attracted to this artwork, and they provided it with elegance and connotation, so that it had a fascinating charm.

Refined Scholars and Purple Clay Pot

The improvement of the art of purple clay pot was the joint efforts of artisans and literati of past dynasties. The involvement of literati in particular, gives the teapot a more elegant style and appearance.

In ancient times, enjoying tea and poetry and composing couplets were

•《惠山茶会图》（明 文徵明）
A Tea Gathering in Huishan by Wen Zhenming (Ming Dynasty, 1368-1644)

"雅趣"，参与其事，成为"风雅之举"。明代文徵明曾作《惠山茶会图》，画出了古代文人以茶会友的浪漫。

宋代大诗人苏轼一生嗜茶，他曾在《试院煎茶》一诗中表露："且学公家作茗饮，砖炉石铫行相随"。这里的"铫"便是一种烧水用的小型吊壶，与后世的紫砂提梁壶极为相似。经专家分析，"石铫"中的"石"并非"石头"，极有可能就是指紫砂一类的材质，而

highlights of social gatherings of literati. Outstanding poems and paintings about tea therefore came forth in great number. Purple clay pot and literati share something in common, that is, simplicity, pureness and integrity. The appreciation of teapots by literati is considered a graceful hobby, while their involvement in teapot making is deemed a refinement. Wen Zhengming of the Ming Dynasty depicted this elegant practice in his painting *A Tea Gathering in Huishan*.

Su Shi, a famed poet of the Song Dynasty (960-1279), was a tea enthusiast over his life. In his poem "Tea Brewing in Examination Hall" he referred to a kind of tea ware, and the poem reads "For the time being, I will follow those officers, to carry a stove and stone *Diao* with me." Here *Diao* is a kind of small teapot, rather similar to those with upper handles of later periods. Also, according to experts, the stone *Diao* may well have been made from a type of soil, like purple clay. In this respect, the stone *Diao* may most probably be a purple clay pot. Again, a folk legend spread in Yixing: "Su Shi had designed a kind of teapot with a three-branch upper handle, which is still in use nowadays, and is named 'Dongpo Upper Handle Teapot' ".

The famous "Eight Eccentrics of Yangzhou" of the Qing Dynasty (1616-1911), namely Luo Pin, Li Fangying, Li Shan, Jin Nong, Huang Shen, Zheng Xie, Gao Xiang and Wang Shishen, being either calligraphers or painters or both, were fond of tea and teapots. They attached great importance to tea drinking and appreciation. Zheng Xie in particular was a passionate lover of purple clay pots. He spoke of the teapot in his poem "A Tiny Garden of the Li Family":

Sweeping the yellow leaves and brewing the autumnal tea leaves, this was

"石铫"很可能就是紫砂壶。在宜兴流传着苏轼曾设计过一种提把为三叉的提梁壶的故事，这种壶式一直沿用至今，被称作"东坡提梁壶"。

清代著名的"扬州八怪"，即书画家罗聘、李方膺、李鱓、金农、黄慎、郑燮、高翔和汪士慎。他们既是茶友，也是壶友，对饮茶品茗都十分讲究。尤其是"八怪"之一的郑燮（郑板桥），非常喜欢用宜兴紫砂壶泡茶。他在《李氏小园》一诗中曾这样写道：

兄起扫黄叶，弟起烹秋茶。
明星犹在树，灿灿天东霞。
杯用宣德瓷，壶用宜兴砂。
器物非金玉，品洁自生华。

相传郑燮在用壶玩壶过程中，经过反复揣摩，博采众家之长，还亲手制作了一把紫砂壶，并在壶上刻下一首诗：

嘴尖肚大耳偏高，才免饥寒便自豪。
量小不堪容大物，两三寸水起波涛。

the morning of two brothers.

Stars are still hanging in the trees, and a bright glow has appeared in the east.

Teacup was born of Xuande Porcelain, while teapot was made of Yixing Clay.

Though not as precious as gold and jade, they send out pure and noble rays.

It is said that in the course of his using and appreciating the teapot, Zheng Xie, through repeated study and learning widely from others, had personally produced a tea pot and engraved a poem on it:

Mouth sharp, belly big, ears too high, no sooner get rid of cold and hunger than take pride.

The capacity is too small to hold something great, and a small spray can set off waves inside.

● 《烹茶洗砚图》（清 钱慧安）
Brewing Tea and Washing Inkstone by Qian Hui'an (Qing Dynasty, 1616-1911)

雅器与雅商

紫砂壶是"雅器",并非单纯的商品,与紫砂壶打交道的商人,也大多是颇有文化内涵的"雅商"。说起钟爱紫砂壶的雅商,就不得不提到明代的江南富商沈万三。

相传有一天,沈万三家门口来了一个衣衫褴褛的老乞丐。他与一般的乞丐有所不同,颇有些仙风道骨,而且讨饭的家伙竟然是一把大口紫砂壶。沈万三是个壶痴,一见到这把紫砂壶就眼前一亮,忙问乞丐是否卖壶,不料被乞丐一口回绝。沈万三于是将老乞丐留下,奉他为沈府的贵宾。此后几年里,沈万三一直好好地招待这个老乞丐,还经常邀请他一起品茶,借机把玩那把紫砂壶。后来,老乞丐终于在寿终正寝之前将紫砂壶送给了沈万三。

Elegant Wares and Merchants

The purple clay pot is an elegant ware but not a simple product, and the merchants dealing with it are mostly well-cultured. Speaking of merchants who favor purple clay pots — Shen Wansan, a wealthy businessman of the Ming Dynasty has to be mentioned.

Legend has it that one day, a ragged old beggar came over to the gate of Shen Wansan's mansion. He was somewhat different from ordinary beggars, behaving quite like a nobleman. The ware he was using to beg turned out to be a big-spout purple clay pot! Shen, being an expert and enthusiast, was immediately attracted by this pot, and hurriedly asked if the beggar would sell it but was refused. Shen, however, did not give up. He invited the beggar to stay at his house and treated him as an honored guest. In the years that followed, Shen was very kind to the beggar, sharing tea time with him while taking the opportunity to appreciate the teapot, and later, the old beggar finally gave the pot to Shen before he came to an end.

诗画与紫砂壶

紫砂壶之所以文化内涵深厚,主要因为它集中国传统艺术"诗、书、画、印"于一身。数百年来,紫砂壶上的装饰图案包括诗词歌

Poetry, Painting and Purple Clay Pot

Purple clay pot has profound connotations because it combines Chinese traditional art — poetry, calligraphy, painting and seal. Over hundreds of years, artists have cleverly

赋、花鸟、山水及古装人物等等，将中国书画艺术中的元素应用得十分完美。

紫砂壶上的铭文多为古人的诗词歌赋，内容多是与茶或草木有关的题咏，字体则有真、草、隶、篆、魏碑等；绘画题材多为花卉鸟虫，或山水、人物等，表现手法上或工笔或写意，或二者兼具。正因为这些极富文人气息的装饰，才使得紫砂壶能够集雕塑、书画、诗词、印章、篆刻等诸多艺术门类于一体，在民间工艺品中脱颖而出，成为传统艺术中的一枝奇葩。

included the elements of Chinese painting and calligraphy — poetry, flowers and birds, landscapes and costume figures — in the decorative patterns of the teapot.

The inscriptions on the teapot are mostly ancient poetry and chants concerning tea or plants, and the style of writing is inclusive of regular, cursive, official, seal, *Weibei* scripts, etc.; the subject matter of the painting on the pot body generally involves flowers, birds and worms, landscapes or figures, in the manner of *Gongbi* (realistic painting with fine brushwork and close attention to details) or freehand brushwork or both. It is these highly refined decorations that make the purple clay pot stand out in the folk arts and crafts and thereby become a miracle of traditional art.

墨宝壶

　　墨宝壶即是镌刻有著名书画家墨宝的紫砂壶，它集金石、书画、文学为一体，有很高的艺术价值。早在明清时期就出现了墨宝壶，著名的书画家董其昌、郑板桥、陈曼生、任伯年、吴昌硕等都曾经和紫砂壶艺人合作，在紫砂壶上留下了珍贵的墨宝。到了现当代，著名书画家黄宾虹、亚明、唐云、程十发等也在紫砂壶上题字，留下了一批宝贵的墨宝壶。

Mobao Teapot

Mobao teapot refers to those who have calligraphic or painting masterpieces engraved on the body. By incorporating epigraphy, calligraphy, painting and literature, they are of high artistic value. *Mobao* teapot emerged as early as the Ming (1368-1644) and Qing (1616-1911) dynasties. Dong Qichang, Zheng Banqiao, Chen Mansheng, Ren Bonian, Wu Changshuo, among other outstanding artists, all kept their masterpieces on the teapot with the assistance of purple clay artisans. As a continuation, famous artists of modern times including Huang Binhong, Ya Ming, Tang Yun, Cheng Shifa and others too, had their works engraved on the teapots, which were later deemed as treasures.

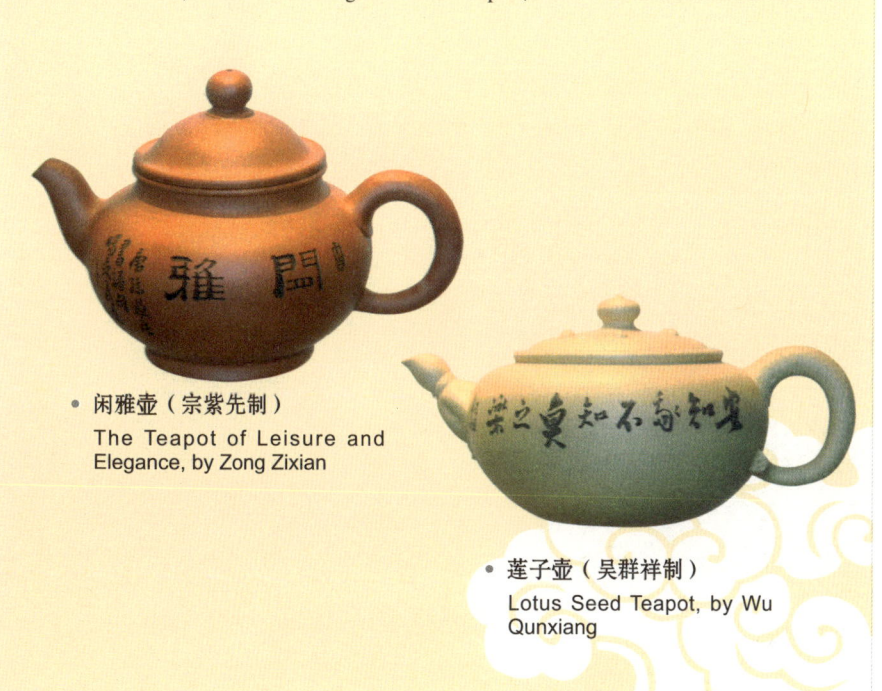

- 闲雅壶（宗紫先制）
  The Teapot of Leisure and Elegance, by Zong Zixian

- 莲子壶（吴群祥制）
  Lotus Seed Teapot, by Wu Qunxiang

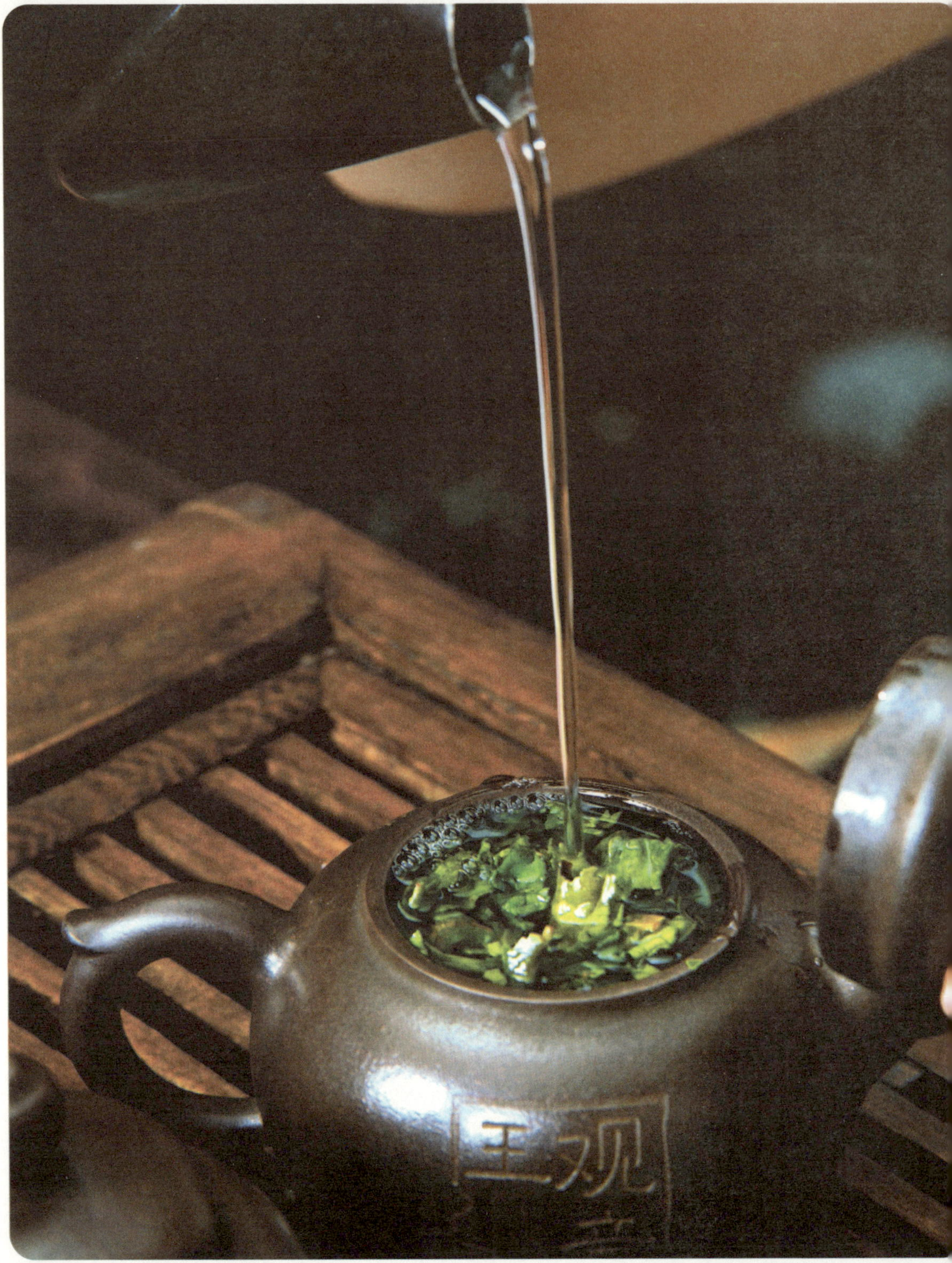
王观

造型之美
Beauty of Appearances

　　作为一件工艺品，紫砂壶的美首先体现在造型上，即材质、颜色、结构和壶式之美。外在的形象和轮廓，是人们对紫砂壶第一眼的观感印象。紫砂壶的结构虽基本固定，但细微之处却各有不同；壶式虽多种多样，但又自有其规律在内。

As a work of art, the beauty of the purple clay pot lies first in its appearance, namely, texture, color, structure and shape, since what greets people first is the external image and shape of a teapot. The structure and shape of the teapot are different, but generally rule-based.

> 独一无二的泥中泥

"人间珠玉安足取，岂如阳羡一丸土。"这句诗描写的就是紫砂泥，它是宜兴所特有的一种陶土。紫砂泥不仅色彩丰富，且细腻柔韧，烧后坚硬光滑，叩之有金属声。

紫砂泥约在2亿—4亿年前就形成了，深埋于山腹之中，被当地人开采出来制陶。紫砂泥的原生形态与常见的胶泥、黄土并不相同，它深埋于岩石层中，呈片状结构矿石态，杂生于夹泥矿内，所以，紫砂泥又有"岩中之

- 朱泥矿石
  Zhuni (Cinnabar Clay) Ores

> Clay of Clay—a Unique Character

"Are jade and jewelry in this world really that good? A pill of clay in Yangxian dwarfs them all." The verse was used to describe purple clay — a unique mud produced only in Yixing. Purple clay is not only colorful but delicate and flexible. When fired, it becomes hard and smooth, and gives a metallic sound when tapped.

Buried deep underground, purple clay formed about 200-400 million years ago and was mined by local people to make ceramics. The purple clay is different from ordinary mud and loess in terms of native form. It is a kind of flaky-structure mineral located within mud ores

紫砂泥片
Slices of Purple Clay

岩""泥中泥"之称。紫砂泥的主要矿物质成分是水云母、高岭石、云母屑、石英以及铁、铜、铯等十几种微量元素，其中石英颗粒就是紫砂泥的"砂"。

"砂"是人们喜爱紫砂器的主要原因。紫砂器的质感、肌理、色泽，都要由"砂"体现出来。紫砂器在经高温烧成之后，残留的石英等矿物质形成了断断续续的气孔群，紫砂器因此具有透气而不漏水的特性，既没有土气，又不易变形。使用的年代越久，壶身色泽就愈加光润古雅，泡出来的茶汤也就越醇郁芳馨。

紫砂壶的美不依赖于任何釉

buried deep in rock layers, hence it is nicknamed "Clay of clay or rock of rock". Chemically, purple clay is a mixture of mica, kaolinite and quartz as well as dozens of trace elements, like iron, copper, cesium, etc., among which quartz plays an important role due to its sandy texture.

"Sand or quartz particle" is one of the main reasons that people love purple clay wares, and the texture, vein and color of these wares are reflected in the "Sand". After firing at a temperature of 1150 degrees Celsius, the leftover quartz and other minerals form an intermittent group of pores, permeable by air but not water. The fired ware comes with no earthy odor and will not be easily deformed. After prolonged use, the teapot delivers a smooth and elegant color, while giving the tea soup more fragrance. When used exclusively for one kind of tea for a long time, boiling water alone in it will bring out the fragrance of tea.

The glamour of purple clay pot comes from its natural color instead of any glaze. The rich colors of clay carn it the reputation of "Colorful Soil". Normally, purple clay consists of *Zini* (purple clay), *Hongni* (red clay) and *Lvni* (green clay).

色，即使以砂色本身示人，也会呈现多样的色彩。根据颜色，紫砂泥主要分为紫泥、红泥和绿泥三种。

紫泥

紫泥位于紫砂矿的夹层中，主要产于丁蜀镇黄龙山。所谓夹层是指夹于地层中，深埋在泥土下受自然压力形成的坚硬的块状岩泥层。紫泥主要成分为水云母，并含有不等量的高岭土、石英、云母屑及铁

Zini (Purple Clay)

Located in the intercalary strata of purple clay ores, *Zini* is produced mainly in Huanglong Mountain, Dingshu Town. To put it simply, *Zini* is sandwiched between heavy sedimentary rock formations, and is mainly composed of water mica, and contains a different amount of kaolin, quartz, mica chips, iron, etc. The raw material is purple or purplish red, with light green spots. When fired, the appearance presents a color of purple,

- 素身壶（紫泥）
Mono-color Teapot (*Zini*)

- 茄段壶（紫泥）
Egg Plant-shaped Teapot (*Zini*)

• 三足石瓢壶（紫泥）
Three-legged Gourd Teapot (*Zini*)

质等成分。紫泥原料呈紫色或紫红色，并带有浅绿色斑点，烧后外观可呈紫色、紫棕色或紫黑色。

由于紫泥的属性近似于制瓷原料，可塑性很好，泥坯强度高，干燥收缩率小，具有优良的工艺性能，因此是制作紫砂壶最主要的泥料。紫泥还可以分为梨皮泥、淡红泥、淡黄泥、密口泥、天青泥、清水泥等品种。

红泥

红泥因其含铁量多寡不等，烧成之后呈朱砂色、朱砂紫或海棠红等色。朱泥是红泥中的精品，产量很小，早年除销往南洋的"水平

purplish brown or purplish black.

Similar to porcelain clay, *Zini* is characterized by perfect plasticity, small shrinkage and high-strength clay body, which makes it the ideal raw material for purple clay pots. Further, *Zini* can be further divided into pear-skin clay, pink clay, yellow clay, dense mouth clay, grey clay, clear clay and so on.

Hongni (Red Clay)

The varied amount of iron content in *Hongni* produces wares with cinnabar, cinnabar purple or Begonia in color. Among *Hongni*, *Zhuni* (cinnabar clay) is the top grade. With very limited quantities, *Zhuni* is normally applied as decorative material painted on purple

● 金瓜壶（朱泥）
Melon Teapot (*Zhuni*)

● 大红袍壶（朱泥）
Grand Red Robe Teapot (*Zhuni*)

小壶"用朱泥制坯外，一般只用做化妆土，涂在紫砂泥坯上，作为装饰。后来，有制壶艺人为求得更精细的泥料，将朱泥进行洗泥、沉淀，得到了质地细如滑脂的泥料，这就是朱泥胎土。朱泥的含铁量在18%左右，烧成后壶身呈红色。朱泥的泥性甚娇，成型难度亦大，一般成品率仅七成，故朱泥不宜制作大件器物，只能制作中小件器物。

由于朱泥细腻滋润，含铁量高，耐温低，烧结后的密度和玻化程度都高，吸水率又低，因此是质地最致密的紫砂泥品种。

绿泥

绿泥略带青灰色，如青壳鸭蛋的

clay bodies, except for those tiny teapots sold to Southeast Asia in early years. Later, *Zhuni* is further extracted by some artisans into finer and smoother clay material. *Zhuni* has an iron content of around 18%, and it shows vermilion after firing. Not as hard as other clay, it is hardly intended for large-sized articles due to the difficulties in techniques.

However, *Zhuni* is the kind of clay with the finest particle size. Delicate, moist and high in iron, it can be fired at low temperatures to produce wares with high density and vitrification as well as low water absorption.

Lvni (Green Clay)

Being slightly greyish green, green clay resembles the color of a duck eggshell,

颜色,烧成后多呈米黄色。绿泥泥质较嫩,耐火力也比紫泥略低,一般多用做胎身外面的粉料或涂料,以使紫砂陶器皿的颜色更为多彩。

紫泥、红泥、绿泥这三种紫砂泥产于不同的陶土矿层,经过加工,烧成后为"本色壶"。但经工匠们巧妙搭配后,成品可烧成海棠红、朱紫砂、葵黄、墨绿、白砂、淡墨、梨皮、豆青、新铜绿等多达几十种的颜色,并且全凭原料呈现的天然色泽,显得质朴高雅。现如今的缎泥就多属于调配泥,并不是泥矿开采出来的单一品种泥料,而是由紫泥和绿泥调配出来的。

and generally shows beige after firing. In terms of hardness, green clay is somewhat tender and of low endurance of fire. Therefore it is often used to decorate the outer surface of the clay body, to provide clay wares with multiple colors.

Zini, *Hongni* and *Lvni* belong to different argil beds. Their natural colors when fired can be enriched and altered through various mixing procedures. The finished products come in as many as dozens of colors including Begonia red, cinnabar purple, stock yellow, dark green, white sand, light black, pear-skin, patina green, and others, all of which present the natural color of raw materials, appearing simple and elegant. Principally, today's *Duanni* is a mixture of green and purple clay instead of a single variety.

- 金文砖方壶(缎泥)
Brick-shaped Teapot (*Duanni*)

- 诗文传炉壶(缎泥)
Teapot with Painting and Poetry (*Duanni*)

紫砂泥的开采和提炼

紫砂泥的开采、加工和配置程序都十分复杂，每一道工序均须严格把关，方能取得上等的紫砂泥。紫砂泥的开采针对不同品种、不同地质条件，主要有两种方式，即明掘、暗掘。

明掘只需掘去1—2米的表层废土，即可采到紫砂泥。暗掘则需要先凿矿井，穿过黄石岩层，或在黄石岩层凿出横穿式隧道至泥层，然后才能进行开采。

刚刚开采出来的紫砂泥是不能直接使用的"生泥"，需要经过一番处理才可使用。处理手段主要包括"炼泥""陈腐""澄泥"和"踏炼"几种。

生泥的外形如同块状岩石，分拣出来后堆放于露天中自然风化。待泥块松散变成小块时，便可将泥料捶碎，经过筛选，再加水调和，然后人工脚踩踏炼，这就是"炼泥"。等到泥料软硬适中时，用铁铲切成大小适当的方块，放置在阴湿的地窖中进行"陈腐"，经常洒水，以保持泥的湿度。"陈腐"的时间越长越好，当泥中的有机物成分全都腐烂挥发后，可提高成品烧制的质量。古代紫砂艺人特别重视"陈腐"。据说"陈腐"达到百年的纯紫砂泥，价格贵过黄金。

澄泥即将泥料经过粗碎，然后用水浸润，再进行除水、澄淀等一系列处理步骤。踏炼一般用于缸、瓮等日用粗陶泥料的处理，包括将泥料摊晒、捶碎、过筛、加水调和、脚踏踩炼、用木杆切碎等步骤。

从矿砂到泥料是一个大浪淘沙的过程，一般情况下，50千克好的矿砂仅能提炼出3~3.5千克的好泥料，炼泥率不足10%。

- 用河水冲洗提纯紫砂泥
Washing and refining purple clay

Mining and Refining of Purple Clay

Mining, processing and combining purple clay involve very complex procedures. Each procedure must be strictly done in order to obtain superior clay. The ways of excavation vary according to clay varieties and geological conditions, shallow dredging and deep dredging being the common approaches.

Shallow dredging is to simply remove the topsoil of one to two meters in thickness below which purple clay is located, while deep dredging is much more complicated, involving mine and tunnel digging and rock penetration.

The clay just excavated is a kind of "raw mud" and is not to be directly used until fully processed. *Lianni*, *Chengni* and *Talian* are common ways to process the clay.

Raw clay looks like a block of rock. After being stored in the open air, it decomposes into grains. Ground by machines into powder and mixed with water, the clay is then to be trodden by someone under their feet. This process is "*Lianni*". Repeat this procedure until the clay material is in moderate hardness, then use a shovel to cut it into cubes of appropriate sizes to place it in a damp cellar for decay. Regular watering is needed to maintain the soil's moisture; perform the decay process as long as possible, so as to make all the organic components in the clay volatile and rotten, which can improve the quality of firing. Ancient artisans paid special attention to the "Decay" procedure; it is said that the pure purple clay, having undergone a hundred years of decay, is more precious than gold.

Chengni is to immerse the roughly crushed clay material in the water and then remove the impurities by precipitation, while *Talian* is normally employed in refining coarse clay for making urns and jars, the procedures of which include air drying, crushing, sifting, mixing with water, treading under feet, shredding and so forth.

It is very complex to make mud ores into clay material. Generally, a mere 3 to 3.5 kg of clay material can be extracted from as much as 50 kg of ores.

- 紫砂泥矿挖掘后的场景
  An Excavating Site of Purple Clay Ores

紫砂泥的配色

　　不同颜色的紫砂泥按照一定的配比调和后，就会形成其他颜色的泥料；紫砂壶在烧制的过程中，窑火的温度及时间长短也会影响紫砂壶的颜色。现代紫砂壶较多地使用着色剂配色，即在泥料中加入着色剂（金属氧化物），烧成后的颜色更是多种多样。经过调和的紫砂泥，颜色有铁青、天青、栗色、猪肝、黯肝、紫铜、海棠红、朱砂紫、水碧、沉香、葵黄、冷金黄、梨皮、香灰、青灰、墨绿、桐绿、鼎黑、棕黑、榴皮、漆黑等，多达上百种。

　　早在明清时期，紫砂艺人就已开始对泥料进行配色处理了。配泥是制壶工匠的一项绝活，全凭制壶人的经验，他们各有绝技，秘不相传，这也是每个工匠所制之壶风格各异的主要原因。

Color Combination of Purple Clay

Purple clay of different colors, combined according to a certain ratio, will form clay material of new colors. In the firing process, time and temperature will also affect the color of purple clay pot. For modern teapots, as much as a hundred varieties of colors are generated through the addition of various metal oxides to the clay material, including azure, maroon, liver, dark liver, copper, Begonia Red, Cinnabar purple, amethyst, aloe, sunflower yellow, etc.

　　As a unique technique, color combining was performed by artisans on clay material as early as the Ming (1368-1644) and Qing (1616-1911) dynasties. It totally relied on an artisan's experience and because of this it has long been considered a trade secret. This is also why each artisan has his own style of making teapots.

- **葫芦壶（储集泉制）**
  此壶泥色奇特，外形为葫芦造型，上绘藤蔓，美妙绝伦。
  Gourd Teapot, by Chu Jiquan
  This gourd-shaped teapot, decorated with beautiful vines, shows a unique color.

> 紫砂壶的结构

紫砂壶的基本结构包括壶身、壶盖、壶嘴、壶把和器足，每一部分单独成型，最后粘接在一起便构成一把完整的紫砂壶。无论是何种风格、何种类型的紫砂壶，都少不了这几种基本要素。

> The Structure of Purple Clay Pot

Basically, the purple clay pot consists of the body, the lid, the spout, the handle and the base, each part being molded individually and attached all together to be a finished product. This applies to teapots of all styles and shapes.

壶盖
The Lid

壶嘴
The Spout

壶把
The Handle

壶身
The Body

器足
The Base

- 紫砂壶的基本结构
  Basic Structure of Purple Clay Pot

壶身

　　壶身是紫砂壶的主体，也是一把紫砂壶最显眼的部分，其作用是盛装茶水。紫砂壶的壶身有许多种样式，不同的壶式就有不同的壶身。壶身的时代特征很明显，一般来说，年代越早，壶身越大。明代的紫砂壶，壶身稍大，造型沉稳大气；清代的紫砂壶则壶身偏小，以小壶居多。

• 当代紫砂壶
Purple Clay Pot of Modern Times

The Body

The principal and most prominent part of a teapot, the body is used to hold water. The numerous styles of the body are partnered with appropriate shapes. The body is of obvious characteristics of the times, generally speaking, the earlier, the bigger. Teapots of the Ming Dynasty (1368-1644) often have big bodies, steady and dignified, while those of the Qing Dynasty (1616-1911) are somewhat smaller.

The Lid

The lid of a teapot falls mostly into three classes — embedded type, cover type and truncated type. Embedded Type refers to the lid sunk into the lip of the opening of a teapot; Cover Type is the one laid over the opening, with a diameter slightly larger than the external diameter of the opening; Truncated Type is to cut off the upper part of a teapot to be used as a lid, with the cross-section as the opening, the two parts meeting seamlessly to form a whole body. Due to the difficulties in techniques, truncated type is only applied in top-grade teapots.

　　A fired teapot should meet certain requirements to make the lid and the

壶盖

　　紫砂壶的壶盖主要有嵌盖、压盖、截盖三种形式。嵌盖是指壶盖陷入壶口内；压盖是指将壶盖覆压于壶口之上，盖的直径要略大于壶口的外径；截盖是指在制坯时，将紫砂壶上端口盖相应的部位切割开来，截下部分做成盖，壶身切口做成壶口，盖合后外形完整。由于制作难度大，只有中高档紫砂壶才会采用截盖设计。

opening: straight, tight, orderly and suitable. "Straight" means that the flange of the lid should be made in a very straight shape so that when serving tea, the lid will not fall off. "Tight" indicates that the lid should fit snugly into the opening. "Orderly" means circular lid and opening must be well structured and easy to turn. "Suitable" stands for the lid used on veined or square pots should be able to open and close smoothly, with the patterns and veins perfectly matched. In addition, regardless of the style of purple

• 压盖
Cover-type Lid

• 嵌盖
Embedded-type Lid

• 截盖
Truncated-type Lid

• 鸡形盖纽
A Knob in Shape of Rooster

• 宝珠形盖纽
A Knob in Shape of Pearl

• 桥形盖纽
A Knob in Shape of Bridge

一把紫砂壶制作完成，口和盖的配合应达到"直、紧、通、转"四点要求。"直"即盖的子口要做得很直，举壶斟茶时，壶盖不会脱出；"紧"即盖与口之间要做到严丝合缝，盖启自如；"通"即圆形的口和盖，必须圆得极其规正，盖合时才能旋转顺畅；"转"即方形紫砂壶和筋囊货的口盖，盖合时可随意盖合，纹形丝毫无差。此外，任何壶式的紫砂壶，壶盖上都要开一个内大外小的喇叭形小孔，这样才不易被水汽糊住，以便于注茶。

壶盖上通常有盖纽，多与壶体配套，造型精致雅观，主要有宝珠形、桥形、牛鼻形、瓜柄形、树桩形和动物形等。盖纽的形状主要取决于壶体的造型，一般圆壶多用宝珠形纽，扁壶多用桥形纽，仿生壶则用瓜柄纽、树桩纽等。

壶嘴

壶嘴是紫砂壶非常重要的组成部分，因为它关系到出水是否畅通。紫砂壶的壶嘴制作非常讲究，长短、粗细及安装位置都需要注意。此外，壶嘴内壁必须光滑畅

clay pot, there must be a trumpet-shaped hole one the lid, large outside and small inside, so that the lid will not easily be sucked by vapor.

The knob of a teapot is often found on the lid, and it is highly compatible with the pot body and of exquisite and compact shape. It appears as something like a pearl, bridge, bovine snout, melon handle, tree stump, animal, etc. The shape of the knob is decided by the appearance of the teapot. Normally, a pearl-shaped knob is partnered with a round teapot, and bridge-shaped for a flat pot, melon pedicle and tree stump for pots in the shapes of animals, organic objects, etc.

The Spout

The spout is a very important part of a teapot as it is crucial for fluent water passing. The making of the spout demands great skills: the length, thickness and position of the spout should be appropriate; the inner wall must be smooth and clear to let water out fluently; when one stops pouring water, a good spout will not drop or drip. For teapots of the Ming Dynasty (1368-1644), the junction of spout and teapot, where water comes out, is of single-hole type, and is

通，出水流畅，收水时不滴水、不流涎。明代的紫砂壶壶嘴根部的出水眼多为独眼，因而易被茶叶堵塞；清代中期开始，出水眼改为网眼式，出水更为顺畅。

紫砂壶的壶嘴可分为一弯嘴、二弯嘴、三弯嘴、直嘴和流五种基本式样。一弯嘴形似鸟喙，故又名"一喙嘴"，顾名思义是指壶嘴只有一个弯；二弯嘴的根部较大，出水畅快，用于一般样式的紫砂壶；三弯嘴的造型古朴高雅；直嘴简单实用；流又叫"鸭嘴"，近代才开始流行，多用于咖啡具、奶杯，茶具中使用相对较少。

easy to be stuck by tea leaves. Since the mid-Qing Dynasty, it was made into a net shape to pass water more smoothly.

The spout of a teapot is divided into five basic types: Single Curve, Double Curve, Triple Curve, Straight and *Liu*. As the name suggests, Single Curve refers to the spout with only one curve, which is also called "Beak Spout" for the fact that it resembles bird's beak. Double Curve spout has a larger junction with the pot body, which makes smoother water passing. It is commonly employed in ordinary teapots. Triple Curve spout features plain and elegant appearance. Straight spout is both simple and practicable. *Liu*, also known as "Duck

- 一弯嘴
Single Curve Spout

- 二弯嘴
Double Curve Spout

- 三弯嘴
  Triple Curve Spout

- 直嘴
  Straight Spout

- 流
  Liu

壶把

壶把是为便于握壶而设的装置，一般位于壶肩至壶腹下端，与壶嘴分别安装在壶体的两侧。紫砂壶的壶把主要分为端把、横把、提梁三种基本式样。

大多数紫砂壶采用端把，呈耳朵状，端握非常方便。横把安装在壶身上，与壶嘴对称，圆筒形壶上

Beak", became popular only in recent times; it is often intended for coffee and milk while rarely seen on teapots.

The Handle

Made for one to carry the pot, the handle is usually located between the pot shoulder and the lower part of the belly, on the opposite of the spout. It comes with three main types — the side handle,

多用横把。提梁是壶把的一种特殊式样，安装在壶体的上方，形式多样，具有很强的装饰作用。提梁还可分为硬提梁和软提梁两种。硬提梁与壶身连在一起，成为整体，其优点是形式感强，透出一种高雅之气，缺点是所占空间较大。软提梁又称"活络提梁"，是制坯时在壶的肩部做一对用来安装提梁的系纽。壶烧成后，用金属丝、管、细藤条、细竹根等做成半圆环，装在系纽上制成。软提梁的优点是壶把可拆卸，便于包装运输。

the horizontal handle and the upper handle.

Side handle is in the shape of an ear, appears on most of the teapots and is easy for one to carry. Horizontal handle is installed symmetrically to the spout, and is commonly seen on round teapots. As a particular style, the upper handle is mounted overhead on a teapot. It comes in great varieties and is highly decorative. Upper handle is further divided into hard handle and soft handle; the hard handle is fixed to the teapot as an indivisible part, which reveals a sense

- 端把
Side Handle

- 横把
Horizontal Handle

- 提梁
Upper Handle

器足

器足是紫砂壶底部的承重部位，其设计直接关系到紫砂壶能否放置平稳，还会影响紫砂壶的美观，因此历代制壶工匠都十分重视器足的设计和制作。

紫砂壶的器足主要分为一捺底、加底和钉足三大类。一捺底，即实际上没有足，是壶身的自然结束，为了搁放平稳，底部是向上鼓起的，多用于圆形紫砂壶，造型简洁灵巧；加底即制坯时在紫砂壶底边附上一道泥圈；钉足是为了使器形不呆板，趋向活泼，搁放平稳。制壶工匠在制坯时会结合每一种壶式的特点而选择相应的器足，由于壶式众多，所以从这三大类中又衍

- 一捺底
Flat Base

of elegance but occupies a relatively larger space. Soft handle, also named "movable handle", is attached to a pair of knobs made on the shoulder of the clay body. Appearing as half circle, this kind of handle is often made of metal wires and pipes, fine rattan, and bamboo roots, and then attached to the fired teapot. In comparison with hard ones, soft handle is detachable and is easy to pack and ship.

The Base

As a load-bearing part, the base is not only of great importance to the secure placement of the teapot but can affect its appearance, and is thus given great attention to by artisans of past dynasties.

The base of the teapot falls mainly into three categories: flat, rimmed and footed. The flat base appears mostly on round teapots. To keep the pot steady, the base is recessed. "To rim" is to place a clay circle on the bottom edge of the clay body. The footed base is intended to give the teapot a more vivid and lively appearance while offering a secure placement for the pot. When shaping the clay body, artisans take into account the shape of the teapot and make an appropriate base. Because of the wide variety of teapot shapes, numerous types

• 加底
Rimmed Base

• 钉足
Footed Base

生出了许多不同类型的器足。明代中期以来，经过历代制壶工匠精心制作的紫砂壶器足，细小的种类已有一千多种。

of bases have been derived from the above three categories. Since mid-Ming, more than a thousand varieties of bases have been created by artisans.

> 紫砂壶的壶式

壶式即紫砂壶的器形。紫砂壶的壶式有很多，但千变万化，离不开最基本的三种壶式，即光货、花货和筋囊货。这三种壶式是紫砂壶各式造型的基础，是紫砂壶实用性和艺术美感相结合的产物。

光货

光货是指壶身为几何体、表面光素的紫砂壶，具有古朴典雅的特点。制作光货的壶坯时，要将器表修饰得极其平整光滑，造型讲究点、线、面的充分结合和平面形态的变化。光货又可分为圆器和方器两大类。

圆器即壶身的横剖面是圆形或椭圆形的紫砂壶。圆器的轮廓由各种方向不同和曲率不同的曲线组

> Shapes of Purple Clay Pot

Although the shapes of purple clay pots are infinite in variety, they all belong to three basic types — the smooth pot, the sculpture pot and the veined pot, all of which are artworks embracing practicability and artistic beauty.

Smooth Pot

The smooth pot refers to those with geometric shapes and smooth, plain surfaces. This kind of pot is characterized by simplicity and elegance. The clay body of this kind requires the surface to be smoothly modified, and stresses the fully integration of dots, lines and facets as well as the variations of facets. Smooth pots can be subdivided into round wares and square wares.

With a round or oval cross-section, the round ware is made up of curves

- 光货——四方壶

  四方壶以高四方体和矮四方体作为壶体。

  Smooth Pot—Square Teapot

  Square teapot features a high or low cubic body.

- 光货——龙蛋壶

  龙蛋壶即蛋形壶，是一种壶身与壶盖整体看起来像一只蛋的紫砂壶。

  Smooth Pot—Egg-shaped Teapot

  When lidded, the teapot looks like an egg.

- 光货——一粒珠壶

  一粒珠是一种传统壶式，特点是壶体为圆球形，无颈，壶盖采用嵌入式结构，盖纽为小圆珠式，三弯嘴，大圆形壶把。

  Smooth Pot—Bead Teapot

  A traditional style, bead teapot features a spherical body without a neck. The lid is of embedded type, and the knob appears as a bead. The spout has three curves while the handle is circular.

- 光货——仿古壶

  仿古壶以仿鼓壶为原型，这种传统壶式有固定的基本形态：壶身扁圆，腹鼓，有短颈，圆弧盖，扁圆纽，二弯嘴，圆形耳把等。

  Smooth Pot—Archaized Teapot

  Modeled on the drum shaped pot, this traditional-style teapot comes with fixed basic forms: oblate body, bulging belly, short neck, circular lid, oblate knob, double-curved spout, round ear-shaped handle, etc.

造型之美 Beauty of Appearances

成，讲究骨肉挺匀，比例恰当，转折圆润，隽永耐看，具有一种活泼柔顺的美感。在制作圆器时要遵循"圆、稳、匀、正"的原则，"圆"即圆润，"稳"即视觉上的平衡和放置的平稳，"匀"即形体上的匀称，"正"即体态周正不歪斜。

方器即壶身的横剖面是四方、六方、八方等方形的紫砂壶。方器的轮廓由平面和平面相交所构成的棱线组成，讲究"方中寓圆"，线面挺括平整，轮廓分明，突出明快挺秀的阳刚之美。

传统的光货包括掇球壶、仿古壶、汉扁壶、四方壶、六方壶、长方壶、传炉壶、僧帽壶等。

花货

花货又称"塑器"，是以浮雕、半浮雕、堆雕等雕塑技法为主要制壶手段，以自然界动植物形象为造型基础制出的紫砂壶。

花货属于仿生器形，又可分为三类：第一类是仿植物的，如梅段壶、松段壶、竹段壶等；第二类是仿瓜果的，如南瓜壶、佛手壶、藕形壶；第三类是仿动物的，如鱼化

of different directions and degrees of curvature. This kind of ware is appropriate in proportion and smooth in transition, revealing a lively sense of beauty. "Round, Steady, Uniform and Straight" are the principles to be followed when producing round ware. Round means smooth, Steady indicates visual balance and secure placement, while Uniform refers to symmetry on the body and Straight stands for a correct and upright body shape.

The square ware is made up of straight lines with different lengths to form geometric patterns, such as square, hexagon, octagon, etc. The flat surfaces, straight lines, and the clear-cut outline of square ware bring a vigorous interpretation to the teapot.

Traditional smooth pots can be exemplified by ball teapots, archaized teapots, flat teapots, square teapots, hexagonal teapots, monk cap teapots and so forth.

The Sculpture Pot

The Sculpture Pot is meant to imitate the appearances of animals and plants by using such sculpture techniques as relief, bas-relief and high relief.

- 花货——梅段壶

梅段壶，塑一段梅树老干为壶体。壶身贴塑梅枝，繁花盛开，再饰以断枝瘿节，钮、把、嘴皆作梅枝形。

Sculpture Pot—Plum Blossom Teapot

The teapot is the mimicry of the trunk of a plum tree. Branches, blossoms and galls are sculptured to paste onto the body, while the knob, handle and spout are in shape of branches.

- 花货——鱼化龙壶

鱼化龙，源于"鲤鱼跃龙门"的吉祥传说，工艺界常以此题材进行创作，作为科举高中的吉兆物。鱼化龙壶一般为活动龙首钮，龙尾把，鱼龙堆身。

Sculpture Pot—Fish-transfigured-into-loong Teapot

Inspired by the legend of "Carps jumping over the loong gate", the subject matter of this teapot is frequently used by artisans, as an auspicious symbol to bless someone with success in the Imperial Examination. Movable knob in shape of loong head, handle in shape of loong tail and decorations of fish and loong on the body are normally found on this kind of teapot.

- 花货——竹段壶

竹段壶，即塑一段竹筒作为壶体，壶流、壶柄也都塑成竹鞭或竹枝之形，又塑新嫩竹枝自竹鞭或竹枝上长出之态。竹是中国文人最喜欢的几种植物之一，因此许多紫砂艺人都以竹之态为壶形。

Sculpture Pot—Teapot in Shape of Bamboo Stem

As the name suggests, this kind of teapot is meant to imitate the stem of bamboo. The spout, handle as well as the knob are designed to shape like bamboo branches or tender shoot. Exceedingly favored by Chinese literati, bamboo is a common subject matter in making teapot.

龙壶，还有以动物之形为壶嘴、壶把的，也可归入此类。

对于花货来说，无论是工艺、颜色还是创意，都要以自然、和谐为标准。这类紫砂壶造型惟妙惟

Sculpture pots often come in three types: in imitation of plants, fruits and animals. Typical examples include plum blossom pots, pine tree pots and bamboo pots; pumpkin pots, chayote pots and

肖，将制壶工艺与自然形态完美结合。明代的花货较少，清代初期，花货风行一时，以陈鸣远的作品为杰出代表。

筋囊货

筋囊货又称"筋纹器"，制壶工匠将自然界里的瓜棱、花瓣、云水纹等形态饰于壶上，被称为"筋囊"，这种以"筋囊"为基础设计的紫砂壶称为筋囊货。筋囊货是紫砂壶中线条比较多的一种，因此特别讲究线条的流畅，口、身、把、嘴之间的线条要过渡自然。筋囊货

lotus root pots; fish-transfigured-into-loong pots, as well as pots with animal-shaped handles and spouts.

For sculpture pots, techniques, colors and ideas aim at what is harmonious and natural. This kind of teapot combines perfectly the techniques and natural forms. Seldom seen in the Ming Dynasty, it was however all the rage in the early Qing Dynasty, Chen Mingyuan's artworks being the outstanding representative.

Veined Pot

Based on natural forms, the veined pot integrates solid and abstract shapes — melon veins, flower petals, or cloud

- **筋囊货——葵仿古壶**

葵仿古壶以葵花为筋纹，以六瓣葵花筋纹组成壶体，筋纹凹凸有致，十分醒目。

Veined Pot—Archaized Teapot in Shape of Sunflower

The veins on this teapot are made to recall the sunflower petals. Either concave or convex, they are very eye-catching.

- **筋囊货——菊瓣壶**

菊瓣壶以菊花瓣为筋纹，盖、钮与壶身的纹理均有筋纹，要求工艺精确，筋纹如出一辙。

Veined Pot—Teapot in Shape of Chrysanthemum Bud

In imitation of Chrysanthemum petals, the veins are executed on the lid, knob and body of this teapot, which requires precise alignment.

● 筋囊货——莲子壶
Veined Pot—Lotus Seed Teapot

的特点是纹理规则、等分均衡、齐整协调、线条顺畅、自然明快，具有强烈的节奏韵律美。

筋囊货的壶表和壶里一样，都是由生动流畅的"筋囊"构成，口部和壶盖的"筋囊"要上下对应、合缝严密。早期的紫砂壶受铜器、锡器等金属器皿的影响较大，以筋囊货为主，制作筋囊货的杰出艺人有时大彬、李仲芳、徐友泉、沈子澈等。

曼生壶

在紫砂壶的发展历史上，曼生壶是一类极其重要的壶式，它的出现具有里程碑式的意义。曼生壶将制壶工艺与文人风雅完美地结合起来，将紫砂壶的艺术性推向顶峰。

patterns — into an aesthetic experience. This kind of teapot involves numerous and complicated lines, and for this reason requires the lines linking up the opening, the body, the handle and the spout to be smooth in transition. Veined pot is often characterized by neat and balanced patterns, smooth lines, and a natural and lively rhythm.

In and outside such teapots are formed vivid and smooth veins, and those on the lid and on the opening should meet seamlessly and tightly. Purple clay pot of the early period, obviously influenced by metal wares, was dominated by veined pots. Shi Dabin, Li Zhongfang, Xu Youquan and Shen Ziche are among the artisans who excelled in making veined wares.

Mansheng Teapot

During the steady progress of purple clay pots, Mansheng teapots are of extreme importance in all teapot shapes and held up as a milestone. By perfectly combining potting skills and scholarly refinement, Mansheng teapots elevated the artistry of teapot to its peak.

Mansheng teapots were co-produced during the reign of Emperor Jiaqing

- 曼生壶——圆珠壶
  Mansheng Teapot—Round Pearl Teapot

- 曼生壶——井栏壶
  Mansheng Teapot—Well-railing Teapot

- 曼生壶——石瓢壶
  Mansheng Teapot—Teapot of Stone Gourd Ladle

- 曼生壶——扁石壶
  Mansheng Teapot—Flat Stone Teapot

曼生壶产生于清代嘉庆年间，是由文人陈曼生和一群懂书画、金石的幕僚设计，制壶高手杨彭年、杨宝年、杨凤年兄妹等制作的。曼生壶壶式设计中寄寓了文人的巧思和雅趣，并利用壶铭书画将这种文人情趣进一步强化，还根据壶式，分别采用不同的泥质，做出天青、黯肝、朱砂、梨皮、调砂、团泥等颜色肌理。

(1786-1820) by Chen Mansheng — a litterateur, teapot master Yang Pengnian and his brothers, as well as a group of friends who were accomplished in painting, calligraphy and epigraphy. The design of Mansheng teapot are placed the subtle ideas and refined taste of literati, which are further enhanced by the addition of inscriptions, calligraphy and paintings. Also, according to the shapes, different clay materials are employed to

- 曼生壶——半球壶
  Mansheng Teapot—Hemispherical Teapot

- 曼生壶——半瓦壶
  Mansheng Teapot—Half Tile Teapot

- 曼生壶——提梁壶
  Mansheng Teapot—Upper Handle Teapot

　　曼生壶器形简洁凝重，壶式以几何形为主，大致可分为四类：一类是借鉴古代铜器、秦砖汉瓦为壶形，如借鉴铜镜器形的"镜瓦壶"，借鉴铜水吊器形的"石铫壶"，借鉴秦砖汉瓦而设计的"飞鸿延年壶""半瓦壶""砖方壶"等；第二类是借鉴生活用器为壶形，如"合斗壶""柱础壶""井栏壶""台笠壶""钿合壶""合

achieve various colors, like azure, dark liver, cinnabar, pear-skin and so on.

　　The shapes of Mansheng teapots are simple and dignified, and mostly of geometrical types. They are roughly divided into four categories: 1. those following the shapes of ancient bronze wares and tiles of the Qin (221 B.C.-206 B.C.) and Han (206 B.C.-220 A.D.) dynasties, typical examples are "Mirror Teapot" in the shape of a bronze

欢壶"等；第三类是仿动植物形态的壶形，如"匏瓜壶""葫芦壶""圆珠壶""天鸡壶"等；第四类是按照器用功能设计的壶形，如"古春壶""吉直壶""春胜壶"等。此外，曼生壶还有重实用功能的特点，不管器形为何，都可用于沏茶。茶壶的容量大小、高矮尺度、嘴把配置都十分讲究。

曼生壶究竟有多少种，目前并未有定论，经学者研究考据，历代文献中所记载的曼生壶式多达三十八种，有详细图名的就有二十八种。

其他壶式

经过历代艺人的创造和完善，紫砂壶除了花货、光货、筋囊货等三大式样及曼生壶外，还创作出如洋桶、寿星等壶式。紫砂壶发展到现当代，更出现了一些新的造型，如"流线型形体""残缺美形体""色块型形体"等，以及一些特殊壶式，包括微型紫砂壶、鼻烟壶、外销紫砂壶等。

微型紫砂壶如同一颗板栗大小，并无实用功能，只是用于陈设

mirror, "Stonepot Teapot" in the shape of bronze ware, "Square Brick Teapot", etc.; 2. the ones whose shapes are taken from daily objects, like "Plinth Teapot", "Well-railing Teapot", etc.; 3. those in imitation of plants and animals, such as "Gourd Teapot", "Melon Teapot" and "Frog Teapot"; 4. the ones with shapes according to the function of daily utensils, like "*Guchun* Teapot", "*Chunsheng* Teapot" and so forth. Although provided with a great variety of shapes, Mansheng Teapots are highly functional, each kind good for steeping tea, and the capacity, height, the design of lid and spout were given great attention to.

So far there has been no conclusion on how many kinds of Mansheng teapots there would have been. According to researchers, as many as 38 kinds of shapes were recorded in the documents of various dynasties, among which 28 were with illustrations and names.

Other Shapes of Teapot

Aside from smooth pots, sculpture pots and veined pots, there are other types of teapots, such as Bucket Teapot, teapots in the shape of the God of Longevity, etc., owing to the creation and improvement of

龙头一捆竹壶

龙头一捆竹壶的壶体结构和纹样极富中国传统文化意味。

A-bundle-of-bamboo Teapot with Loong Head Spout

The structure and patterns of this teapot are full of traditional Chinese cultural connotations.

和赏玩。微型紫砂壶做工精巧，有的还出自制壶名家之手，堪称紫砂壶中一绝，更因传世甚少，因此极为珍贵。清代制壶名家邵大亨和惠逸公皆有微型紫砂壶作品传世。

外销紫砂壶是清代专门为了出口东南亚各国而制作的紫砂壶。外销紫砂壶在泥料的选配和造型方面变化多样，装饰精美异常，造型偏古朴，出水顺畅。外销紫砂壶多以朱泥制成，采用贴花、镂空、泥绘等手法装饰，大多数壶底印有"贡局"印铭。从明末开始，宜兴

artisans of the past dynasties. In modern times, even more shapes emerged, like "Streamlined Body", "Incomplete Physical Beauty", etc. Also, there are some special types of pots, including mini-teapots, snuff bottles, teapots for sale abroad, etc.

With exquisite workmanship, the mini teapot is about the size of a chestnut, and is intended for appreciation instead of practical use. Some of the mini teapots, hand-made by famed artisans while rarely preserved till today, were considered treasures. Fortunately, the ones by Shao Daheng and Hui Yigong of the Qing Dynasty survived.

Teapots for sale abroad in the Qing Dynasty are the ones to be exported to Southeast Asian countries. They come in a wide variety of clay materials and shapes, are of exquisite decorations, simple shapes and are capable of passing water smoothly. Many of these kinds of

微型紫砂壶
Mini Teapot

便开始生产外销紫砂壶，主要销往日本、东南亚及欧洲诸国。第一次鸦片战争后，西方古董商人纷纷来中国搜罗文物，紫砂壶也在收购之列，于是宜兴的生产者纷纷生产仿古器，扩大了国外市场。

teapots are made of *Zhuni* and decorated in the manner of appliqué, piercing and clay painting. On the bottom an inscription of *Gongju* (meaning this teapot is to be exported) is usually found. Since the late Ming Dynasty, purple clay pots had been exported from Yixing to Southeast Asia and Europe. After the Opium War in 1840, Western antique dealers flooded into China for artifacts inclusive of purple clay pots. Under the circumstances, producers in Yixing went in for the production of archaized wares, and expanded businesses in foreign markets.

• **汉君壶**

汉君壶的器形特点是壶身扁圆，大口斜肩，直壁腹，腹以下又斜收，平底，三弯嘴，扁方形圆形耳，盖采用虚嵌式结构，呈圆弧形凸起，桥形钮。

The Teapot of *Hanjun*

This teapot features an oblate body, a large opening, oblique shoulder and vertically flat belly. The lower part of the belly tilts inward to the flat base. The spout is of triple curve type, looking across the opening to a circular handle; on the bulging, embedded lid is situated the knob in shape of a bridge.

• **四方弧棱壶**

四方弧棱壶壶身以方斗为基本形制，将四条侧棱作圆化处理，同时壶身自方口以下均作弧面鼓出，一直至底。

Square Teapot with Four Round Side Edges

This teapot takes the form of *Dou* (a square vessel used to hold rice), its otherwise angular edges on the four sides are designed to be rounded off, the body bulges from the opening to the bottom base.

鼻烟壶

  鼻烟壶是用来盛装鼻烟的小壶，通常高6—8厘米，小口，有带塞的盖，塞上装有象牙或牛骨制成的小匙，以便挹取鼻烟。清代中期，宜兴紫砂鼻烟壶风行一时，传世作品有泥绘山水鼻烟壶、珐琅釉彩绘鼻烟壶。

Snuff Bottle

The snuff bottle, about 6-8 centimeters in height, is used to store snuff. The bottle has a tiny opening and comes with a stopper, to which a very small spoon made of ivory or bones is attached for extracting the snuff. In the mid-Qing Dynasty, snuff bottles made out of Yixing purple clay became popular. Masterworks of this period included the Clay-painting Landscape Snuff Bottle, and the Color-painting Snuff Bottle with Enamel Glaze.

- 紫砂鼻烟壶
Purple Clay Snuff Bottle

茶宠

  茶宠是用茶水滋养的宠物，多为紫砂工艺品，喝茶时需用汤涂抹或用剩茶水直接滴淋。茶宠最早出现在明代，最初只是为人们在品茶时增添情趣，而后逐渐成为文人雅士们的心爱之物。茶宠同样具有紫砂壶的灵性，只要养得得法，年长日久，便会温润可人，茶香四溢。

  常见的茶宠造型有金蟾、貔貅、辟邪、小动物、人物等，大都寓意招财进宝、吉祥如意。还有一些茶宠内部为中空结构，浇上热水后会产生吐泡、喷水等有趣的现象。

  古人大都喜欢神兽茶宠，诸如青龙、白虎、玄武、朱雀、金蟾、貔貅、长寿龟……由于它们在传说中都有着各自的神通，或辟邪、或镇宅、或旺财、或赐福，所以养茶宠既在于养的情趣，也在于它们所寄予的美好意愿。

Tea Curios

Tea curio is a small gadget nourished by tea soup. Mostly made of purple clay, it is to be sprinkled or drenched directly with leftover tea soup. First appearing in the Ming Dynasty (1368-1644), it was originally meant to add to the fun on tea drinking, and then gradually became a favorite object of literati. Tea curio and purple clay pot share characteristics in some respects. When carefully nursed, its surface grows lustrous and delivers the fragrance of tea with age.

Pixiu (a Chinese mythical hybrid creature, considered to be a very powerful protector), toad and other small animals and figures are among popular tea curios, and many of these gadgets are emblematic of good fortune and luck. Some of the tea curios are hollow inside, and spit bubbles or spout water when sprinkled with hot water.

Tea curios of ancient times often appear as something like loongs, tigers, toads, sparrows, *Pixiu* or tortoise as these animals are symbolic creatures that deliver the goodwill of people.

- 紫砂茶宠
Purple Clay Tea Curios

工艺之美
Beauty of Craftsmanship

  虽然紫砂壶工艺的每一个流派，乃至每一个艺人，都有自己的风格特征，但紫砂壶工艺在整体上有统一的要求。具体来讲，就是要求壶的口盖要平整严密，盖内子口挺直，壶身没有褶皱，壶的重量不能过重或过轻，壶内也要光滑干净，流和把与壶体的衔接自然牢固，端拿舒服，印款清晰。

Different schools and artists have different craftsmanship. Although they have styles of their own, they follow an overall requirement. Specifically, the opening and the lid of a pot should meet tightly and seamlessly, and the flange of the lid should be straight, the inner and outer surfaces of the body are required to be smooth, the weight of the pot should be moderate. Also, the spout and the handle are to be naturally and firmly attached to the body, and the handle should have a good grip and should feel right in the hand. The engraved inscriptions or seals should be clear and recognizable.

制作工艺

数百年来，紫砂艺人们在不断的探索中，发明了一套制作方法，所使用的工具也是名目繁多，数量多达百种。

制作工具

紫砂壶的制作，不仅要靠艺人们精湛的技艺，还必须借助各种工具，二者完美地结合，才能使紫砂壶成型，使它拥有美感与灵性。

紫砂壶的制作工具可分为两大类，一是常用工具，包括木拍子、竹拍子、挖嘴刀、尖刀、矩车等；二是制作某一种造型的壶时配置的专用器具。这些工具一般都由紫砂艺人自己加工、修整而成，其材质有木、竹、石、金属、牛角、皮革、塑料等，形状也各不相同。

The Craftsmanship

For centuries, purple clay artists had invented a set of methods through continuous trials, while the tools involved are of a hundred varieties.

The Tools

The making of purple clay pots as well as their beauty and loveliness rely not only on the superior skills of artisans but also on various tools.

The tools can be divided into two classes: common tools and special tools. The former includes wood beater, bamboo beater, scraper, gauge, and others; the latter are employed in producing the pot with particular shapes. This kind of tool is generally of different shapes and made by the artists themselves, the materials ranging from wood, bamboo, stone, metal to buffalo-horn, leather, and plastic.

• 紫砂壶制作工具
Tools for Making Purple Clay Pot

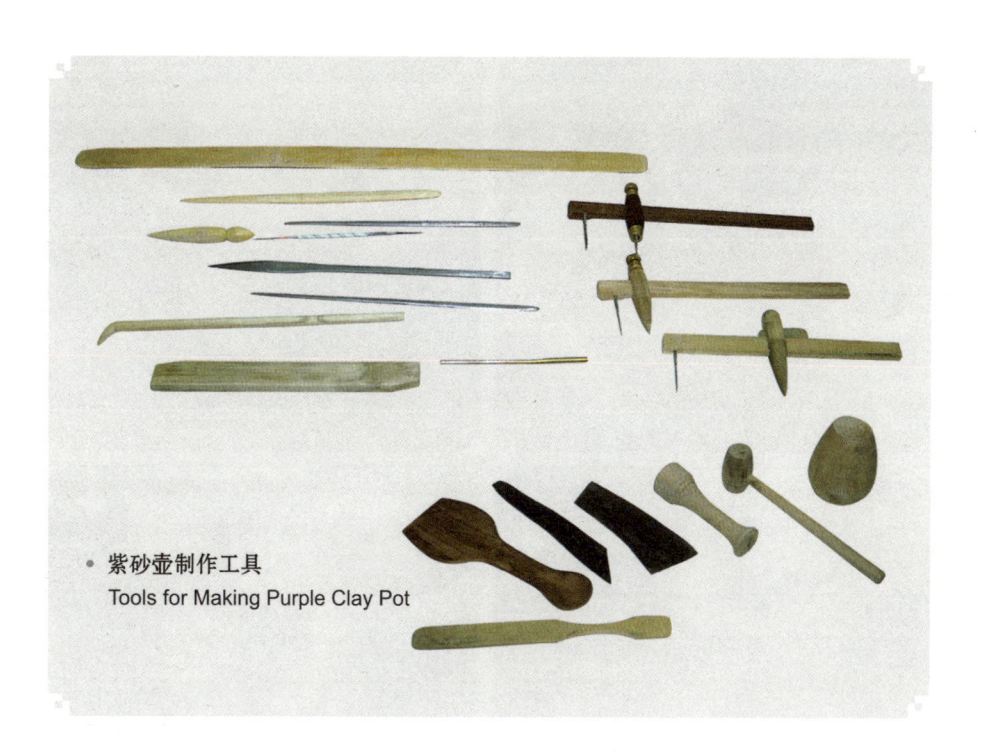

制作方法

　　每一件紫砂壶的诞生，都要经过十到几十道复杂工序。一般来说，紫砂壶采用泥片镶接法成形，即先将湿紫泥拍打成一定厚薄均匀的泥片，分别做出壶的各个部件，再粘接在一起，成为一个壶的雏形；再加以修整、完善，才算制成壶坯。

The Methods

It requires up to dozens of complex procedures to make a teapot. Common practice is as follows: use a beater to beat the wet clay until it is a thin sheet of even thickness; make separately the lid, spout, handle and knob, and then join them together by luting to form a rough model; thereafter, adjustment and modification are needed before a clay body takes shape.

• 艺人正在制作紫砂壶

Artisans in the Process of Making Teapots

从制作的角度上说，紫砂壶分为圆器和方器两大类，制作方法分别为"拍身筒成形"和"镶身筒成形"两种。"拍身筒成形法"主要用于制作圆器；"镶身筒成形法"主要用于制方器和其他几何平面状紫砂壶，如四方形、六方形、长方形、扁方形等。

In terms of production, purple clay pot is comprised of two major types: round wares and square wares. The beating method is often applied to the former, while the mounting method is employed in making square wares and wares of geometrical shapes, like cubic, hexagonal, rectangular, etc.

> 烧制工艺

紫砂壶的烧制方法可分为传统方法和现代方法两大类。传统方法主要是窑烧，烧窑包括龙窑、倒焰窑、隧道窑等；现代方法主要是瓦斯窑烧和电窑烧两种。

龙窑

在古代，紫砂壶的烧制主要依靠龙窑。龙窑是一种依山坡用砖砌筑成的斜坡式的弯状隧道，形状很像一条龙，长度为30—70米，顶端高约12米，倾斜角为8—20度，分窑头、窑床、窑尾三部分。龙窑隧道两旁，每距1.3米开着投放燃料的小洞，俗称"鳞眼洞"。从远处望去，龙窑沿着山坡节节爬行而上，龙身隐约可见几片红土砖块，宛若鳞片，粗糙而又鲜活，展现着最原

> Techniques of Firing

Firing methods can be divided into two classes — the traditional practice and the modern practice. Kiln firing is chiefly applied in traditional practice. The kilns involved include loong kiln, backfire kiln and tunnel kiln. In modern practice, electric kiln firing and gas kiln firing are widely adopted.

Loong Kiln

In ancient times, the firing of purple clay pots was mainly carried out in loong kilns. Made up of bricks, the kiln is a tunnel work generally built along a hill slope, at an angle of about 8-20 degrees, which looks like a loong. It is 30-70 meters long, and consists of the kiln head, the kiln bed and the kiln end, and the top end is approximately 12 meters high. On both sides of the tunnel are opened a number of

始的生命力。当窑火烧起时,最上方的龙尾便会猛烈地吐出红红的火舌,活像一条真龙。

用龙窑烧制紫砂壶时,须先将陶坯装入匣钵(由耐火陶土制成)。每窑可装匣钵约2880只,每个匣钵内可装9把茶壶,因此一窑可烧制紫砂壶约26000件。古人用松枝、硬柴烧窑,烧成温度控制在1200℃左右。一次完整的龙窑烧制至少需要一天一夜,灶口边设有一些很小的观测口,烧制时艺人会凭

small holes at an interval of 1.3 meters, through which firewood can be inserted. Seen from a distance, the kiln steadily crawls up the hillsides, and on the loong body a few slices of red brick loom, just like scales, so rough and fresh that it shows the most primitive vitality. When the kiln fire is lighted, the loong tail on the top end will burst out red flames, conjuring up a real loong.

Before firing in the loong kiln, the clay body is to be placed in a sagger (made of refractory clay), each sagger

- 窑工在清代龙窑旁烧窑的照片(拍摄于1952年)(图片提供:FOTOE)
Kilns Standing Next to a Loong Kiln of the Qing Dynasty during a Firing Session (Taken in 1952)

- **龙窑结构示意图**
  Diagram of Loong Kiln

鳞眼洞：即投柴孔，位于拱顶两侧，沿纵向对称，共两排。
The two rows of firewood holes are located on both sides of the vault, symmetric along a vertical axis.

窑室：即装烧紫砂壶的空间。窑室长度不一，根据其烧制产品的数量和品种而定。
The kiln chamber is used to fire teapots, the length varies according to the number and variety of fired products.

预热燃烧室：位于窑头，呈倾斜炉栅式布局。燃烧室一般长 1.6—2米，宽0.8—1米，高为 0.7—0.8米。
The firing chamber lies at the end of the kiln, with an inclined grate layout. It is normally 1.6-2.0 meters long, 0.8-1.0 meter wide and 0.7-0.8 meter high.

排烟孔：位于窑尾末端的挡烟墙上。排烟孔的面积大小及分布，直接影响窑内温度的传递和烧成时间的长短。
Smoke holes are placed on smoking-stop walls at far end of the kiln. The size and distribution of smoke holes are crucial to the firing temperature and time.

着多年的经验，决定烧窑熄火的时机。这一窑艺术品的成败，就全靠烧窑艺人的智慧了。

宜兴的龙窑历史非常悠久。据考证，早在唐代，那里便有烧制陶器的龙窑了。当代紫砂壶的烧制大都使用电窑，除了个别的龙窑还在使用外，这种传统的烧制方法已淡出人们的视野。不过，全手工制

being able to hold 9 teapots, and about 2,880 saggers being held in a kiln. This amounts to approximately 26,000 teapots fired in one kiln. The ancients used pine branches and hard firewood to fire pottery at a temperature of about 1200 ℃, and it took a day and a night to complete the firing. A few small holes were placed by the stove opening for observation. The firing time, as well as the quality of tea wares, was totally depended on years of experiences of artisans.

古代龙窑遗址
Site of Ancient Loong Kiln

作、经龙窑烧制的紫砂壶在许多艺人及玩家心中仍占有一席之位。因为只有这样的紫砂壶，才是独一无二的，才具备了"土"与"火"的灵性。

The loong kilns of Yixing have a long history. According to research, there had been these kilns as early as the Tang Dynasty (618-907). Today they have been completely replaced by electric kilns except for a few that are still in use. However, purple clay pots fired in the loong kiln are always highly valued by some artisans and collectors for their uniqueness and the spirit dwelling on fire and soil.

前墅龙窑

　　明代的前墅龙窑是宜兴目前仍在使用的唯一一座古龙窑，源源不断地烧制出一批又一批紫砂新壶。前墅龙窑位于宜兴市丁蜀镇前墅村，全长43.4米，窑身外壁宽约3米，内壁底部宽2.3米，高1.55米。窑身左右设有鳞眼洞42对，西侧设装窑用壶口（窑门）5个。

Loong Kiln of Qianshu Village

Dated to the Ming Dynasty (1368-1644), the loong kiln in Qianshu is the only ancient one that's still in use, it produces purple clay pots day in and day out. The kiln is located in Qianshu Village of Dingshu Town, Yixing, and is 43.4 meters in length and 1.55 meters in height. The outer wall is about 3 meters in width, and the bottom of the inner wall is approximately 2.3 meters in width. On both sides of the body are opened 42 pairs of small holes for dropping firewood, on west side of the body are fitted 5 kiln doors.

• 前墅龙窑遗址
Site of Qianshu Loong Kiln

倒焰窑和隧道窑

倒焰窑烧制也是传统的烧窑方法之一,即用煤来燃烧,将热量以对流和辐射的方式传给紫砂壶。倒焰窑的操作管理比较简单,且窑内温度均匀,可以根据紫砂壶器形大小来调节烧成温度。但它以煤或重油为原料,易污染环境,热损耗量大,因此目前已基本被淘汰。

隧道窑烧制也是一种传统的烧窑方法,即采用直线形的隧道来烧制。隧道窑烧制的生产周期短,产量大,成品率高,适合大批量生产,并且能够节约燃料。

Backfire Kiln and Tunnel Kiln

Backfire kiln firing is also a traditional practice, in which coal is used to pass the heat to a teapot by means of convection and radiation. The manipulation of a backfire kiln is simple, and the temperature in the kiln is uniform so that the firing temperature can be adjusted according to the shapes of teapot. What has brought about the elimination of these kilns is that it employs coal or heavy oil which resulted in environmental pollution and severe heat losses.

Still a traditional practice, a tunnel kiln firing is of straight body that is characterized by a short production cycle, high output and rate of finished product, and fuel economy. It is therefore suitable for mass production.

电窑

电窑烧是现代发明的一种通过电热元件把电能转变成热能的新烧窑方法,电窑又称"电阻炉"。电窑结构简单,占地面积小,窑内空间紧凑,热强度高,热能利用率高,窑内陶器不受烟气及灰渣等影响,窑温易于调节监测。

目前宜兴许多个人和小型工

Electric Kiln

Electric kiln firing is a modern practice. Electric kiln is also known as "resistance furnace", in which electrical energy is turned into heat energy via heating elements. With a very simple structure, it is compact while blessed with high thermal efficiency. Pottery in the kiln is kept away from flue gas and ashes, and it is easy to adjust and monitor the firing temperature.

厂都采用箱式电阻炉来烧制紫砂壶。这种电阻炉的电热体靠近炉膛内壁，工作时炉温可达1200℃—1600℃，能烧制不同规格的陶瓷制品。箱式电阻炉适于烧制小批量的大、中、小型紫砂壶。

Currently box furnaces are widely adopted by individuals and small factories in Yixing. The heating element of this kind of furnace is mounted next to the inner wall, so the working temperature can be as high as 1200-1600 degree Celsius, adaptive to various kinds of pottery. The box furnace is intended for firing small quantities of teapots of large, medium and small sizes.

● 小型电窑
Small Electric Kiln

窑变

在烧制紫砂壶等陶瓷器时，会发生一种特殊的现象，即窑变。窑变是指在施釉器皿烧制的过程中，由于釉的组成不同，或者几种釉施于同一器皿之上，从而发生一系列复杂的化学反应所造成的色彩变化。

窑变在瓷器烧制中很常见，因为瓷器要施釉。而一般都是不施釉的紫砂壶，为什么也会出现颜色不一的现象呢？这其中原因有两种，一是火候没有掌握好，使壶的颜色发生了意外的变化，是烧制失败的表现；二是不同颜色的泥料在烧制过程中，由于窑内温度的变化，呈现出不同的颜色和肌理效果，这是真正意义上的紫砂窑变。紫砂壶窑变是一种可遇而不可求的事情，因此发生窑变的紫砂壶，才会异常珍贵。

Furnace Transmutation

Furnace transmutation is a particular case that occurred in the course of firing pottery and porcelain. Specifically, it is an accidental color change resulting from a series of complex chemical reactions in the process of glazing.

Furnace transmutation is very common to porcelain because glazing is required in the firing process, but it is rare to glaze a purple clay pot. Why does this happen in the case of no glaze? There are two reasons: first, the firing time is not well controlled, so that the color of the pot has an accidental change, indicating that the teapot is defective; secondly, clay of different colors, having experienced an obvious change in firing temperatures, renders the teapot with different colors and textures, which is a truly furnace transmutation. Furnace transmutation has unpredictably happened, and because of this, the teapot born in such cases is extremely valuable.

- 宋代窑变釉壶形灯
  Glazed Furnace Transmutation Lamp in Shape of Pot (Song Dynasty, 960-1279)

> 装饰工艺

紫砂壶是集中国传统文化"诗、书、画、印"为一体的艺术品，其艺术价值的高低不仅取决于它的用料和造型，还取决于其装饰工艺。紫砂壶的装饰工艺主要包括线装饰、刻画装饰、泥绘装饰和印贴装饰、彩釉装饰、镶嵌装饰，以及一些特殊装饰技法。

线条装饰

线条装饰是最古老的装饰纹样之一，因其简单、质朴之美得到古往今来人们的喜爱。紫砂壶的装饰便借鉴了这些古老的几何纹样，形成了独特的线条装饰体系。紫砂壶线条装饰的种类有很多，各种各样的线条都必须用牛角或铁、木、竹质的专用线尺工具进行加工。通过

> Decorative Methods

The purple clay pot is a work of art that incorporates poetry, calligraphy, painting and seal carving. Although it is particularly known for its material and shape, there are also a great variety of decoration methods that do credit to it. The decorative methods chiefly involve line decoration, carving decoration, clay painting, pasting and printing, color glazing, tessellation, and some special methods.

Line Decoration

One of the oldest decorative patterns, line decoration is favored by people through the ages for its rustic and simple beauty. This kind of decoration is applied on purple clay pots to form a unique decorative system. There are many varieties of line decorations, all of which have to be processed with

- **抽角线**

抽角线又叫"折角线",用于方形紫砂壶器的面与面的交接过渡,用抽角线或折角线处理的方器,藏锋匿角,方中寓圆,使造型更浑厚,产生多变的光影效果。

Acute-angle Line

The acute-angle line is used on the transition of two faces of square ware. This kind of lines brings a more vigorous appearance and varied lighting effects by rounding off the angles and corners.

- **筋囊线**

筋囊线有云水纹、如意纹、菱纹、花瓣纹等几种,构成壶身筋囊装饰,凹凸弧线,布满器身,流畅贯通。

Veined Line

The veined line is inclusive of cloud patterns, *Ruyi* patterns, lozenge patterns, flower petal patterns, etc. These patterns, convex or concave, straight or curved, cover the whole body of the ware to form the veined decorations.

- **云肩线**

云肩线用于壶颈部、盆类口下沿等转折部分,一般要求轻薄如一片白云,以增强紫砂壶的灵动感。

Cloud Line

The cloud line is applied on the transition of the neck and body of a teapot or somewhere below the rim of the opening of a bowl. It is generally required to be as light and thin as a wisp of cloud, to bring a sense of rhythm.

- **灯草线**

灯草线是状如灯草的小圆线,一般用于紫砂器的口沿、足部,或肩腹部,是器形转折起止的交代,有装饰效果,也可减少烧制时器物的形变。

Rush Line

The rush line is a kind of thin circles used normally on the rim of the opening, around the base or on shoulder and belly. As the beginning or ending of shape transition, the rush line brings a decorative effect and is able to reduce deformation of a teapot in firing session.

- 子母线

子母线是用于壶类的口盖组合处的一粗一细的双线，又称"文武线"，一般处理成上粗下细、上大下小，称为"天盖地"，可增加紫砂壶的厚重感。

Double Line

The double line—one thick and one thin—is used on the rims of opening and lid to lend a sense of dignity to the teapot. These two lines are also called "Civil and Military Lines". Usually the thick one is found on the lid, and the thin one on the opening, and this is named "sky over the earth".

这些线条的转折和过渡，使壶的造型千变万化，不仅加强了紫砂壶的装饰效果，而且可增强泥片粘接处及边缘部分的应力，降低烧制时的残品率。紫砂壶常见的装饰线有灯草线、子母线、云肩线、抽角线、筋囊线等几种。

刻画装饰

刻画装饰是紫砂壶的主要装饰手法之一。它是在制壶工匠署名刻款的基础上发展起来的，且与文人参与紫砂壶设计有关。清代的金石书画家、西泠八家之一的陈鸿

special line rulers made of buffalo-horn, iron, wood and bamboo. These lines are designed variously to create a great variety of shapes. They also give the teapot a more appealing decorative effect, and additionally, make it more robust. Typical lines include rush lines, double lines (one thick and one thin), cloud rim lines, acute-angle lines, veined lines, etc.

Carving Decoration

Carving is one of the principal decorative methods applied on purple clay pots. It evolved from the inscriptions of the potter's name on the pottery piece, and was closely associated with literati who

寿对紫砂壶刻画装饰手法的发展作出了极大的贡献。在他的大力提倡下，紫砂壶身一面镌刻壶铭，另一面刻画诗、书、画的做法逐渐成为定式，使紫砂壶具成为融器形、诗文、绘画、书法、金石于一体的艺术品。

刻画装饰的题材非常广泛，有山水、人物、花鸟、博古、书法、诗文等多种。自陈鸿寿之后，刻画装饰在紫砂壶制作中广泛流行，不少制壶工匠同时也是金石名手，他们将紫砂壶的装饰艺术发挥到了极致。

took an active role in the designing of teapots. Chen Hongshou, an epigraphist, painter and calligrapher of the Qing Dynasty (1616-1911), had made great contributions to carving decorations. He was credited with the popularization of engraving inscriptions, poetry and paintings on the teapot body. Under these circumstances, the purple clay pot became a work of art that combined characteristic shapes, poetry, painting, calligraphy and epigraphy.

Carving decoration involves a great variety of subject matters — landscape, figures, flowers and birds, ancient learning, calligraphy, poetry, to name a few. After Chen, this kind of decoration

- 刻画装饰
  Carving Decoration

泥绘装饰

泥绘装饰起源于中国古代的漆器堆雕工艺，即先将绿泥、朱泥、紫泥、白泥、朱砂泥、乌泥等制成泥浆，后用毛笔蘸上泥浆，在尚有一定湿度的壶坯体上画花鸟或山水，因画面有一定的厚度，犹如薄浮雕，故又叫"堆画"。传统泥绘装饰的内容包括山水、花鸟及诗文，并且均以中国画构图形式入画，使得泥绘紫砂壶显得典雅古朴。

泥绘装饰最早出现于清朝乾隆年间，道光年间最流行。但由于泥浆的黏附力差，泥绘图案易剥落，因此传世的精品较少。

印贴装饰

印贴装饰是紫砂壶的局部装饰，即将制好的带纹样的泥片粘贴到紫砂壶坯上，形成结构严密、纹样精细统一的装饰效果。常见的印贴装饰纹样有如意云纹、蕉叶纹、蝉纹、夔纹、龙凤纹、水波纹等。印贴装饰将中国传统纹样与紫砂艺术相结合，制作出的紫砂壶古色古香。

became highly fashionable. Some of the artisans themselves were celebrated epigraphists, and they had perfected the carving decoration and used it to great effect.

Clay Painting Decoration

A derivative of pile-up painting applied on ancient Chinese lacquer, clay painting is to paint flowers and birds or landscapes with a brush dipped in thin slurry — made from green clay, cinnabar clay, white clay, purple clay, etc. — on the partially dry clay body. The painting is slightly raised above the background to resemble the bas-relief, which is hence also known as "Pile Up Painting". The subject matters of clay painting include landscape, flowers and birds, poetry and prose, and are executed on the purple clay pot in accordance with the composition of Chinese painting, adding an elegant and simple note to the teapot.

Clay painting was first seen during the reign of Emperor Qianlong (1736-1795) and prevailed during the reign of Emperor Daoguang (1821-1850). Few masterpieces survived because of poor adhesion of the slurry that led to the peel-off of the patterns.

● 泥绘装饰
Clay Painting Decoration

● 印贴装饰
Printing and Pasting Decoration

彩釉装饰

彩釉装饰起源于清代康熙年间，当时中国的对外贸易逐渐发展起来，主要的贸易对象转向了欧洲各国。欧洲人崇尚华丽的外观，因此紫砂艺人们开始尝试在紫砂壶上涂彩，从而出现了加釉的紫砂壶。最初紫砂壶是施五彩，以后又出现

Printing and Pasting Decoration

Printing and pasting decoration is applied on certain parts of the purple clay pot. It is to paste the slices of clay with completed patterns onto the clay body. This kind of decoration produces an effect with well-structured patterns fine, uniformed lines. *Ruyi*, banana leaves patterns, cicadas, loongs, water ripples

珐琅彩、粉彩、蓝白彩、点彩等，统称为彩釉装饰。五彩、珐琅彩、粉彩都是易熔釉色料，在紫砂壶成品上画花卉、山水、人物，再入红炉，二次烧成。其中乾隆粉彩紫砂壶非常精细，可与瓷器媲美，是釉

are among the common decorative patterns. A blending of the traditional Chinese patterns and the art of purple clay, printing and pasting decoration gives the teapot an air of antiquity.

Colored Glaze Decoration

Decoration with colored glazes originated in the period of Emperor Kangxi (1662-1722) when China's foreign trade was gradually developed, the main trade partners were turned to Europe, where gorgeous appearance was much favored. In this respect, artisans began to color the purple clay pot, and this eventually brought about the glazed teapot. Multi-colored glaze was initially executed on the teapot, followed by enamel glaze, famille rose glaze, blue and white glaze, drip glaze, etc., and these are collectively referred to as glaze decoration. Multi-colored glaze, enamel glaze and famille rose glaze are fusible materials, which are often used to paint flowers, landscapes and figures on a bisque-fired teapot, the piece is then re-fired to achieve a finished product. Of all the glazed teapots, teapots in famille rose glaze of the Qianlong period enjoy the finest glaze decoration, so fine that they rival that of the porcelains.

● 蓝彩装饰
Blue Glaze Decoration

● 点彩装饰
Drip Glaze Decoration

• 珐琅彩装饰
Enamel Glaze Decoration

• 炉钧釉装饰
Lujun Glaze Decoration

彩装饰壶中的上品。

"炉钧"是一种特殊的釉彩装饰。制作时在紫砂胎周身施满低温铅釉，这样烧成后，在匀净的天蓝色釉面中有细腻而致密的白毫，很有特色。清末民初曾批量生产炉钧装饰的紫砂壶，常见的有炉钧汉方壶、彩釉汉扁壶、彩釉汉方壶等。

描金装饰

描金装饰是一种高成本的工艺，工序非常繁杂。其方法是先在描金的纹样处涂上一层底釉，用750℃—800℃的温度烧成，再将瓷用金水在釉纹上描画，然后用稍低的温度再烧烤一次。制作描金紫砂

Lujun is a particular type of glaze decoration. It is to apply low-temperature lead glaze over the clay body. When fired, delicate and dense white speckles are evenly distributed over the pure blue glaze, which is unique. *Lujun* teapots were mass produced towards the end of the Qing Dynasty, typical examples include *Lujun* Han Square Teapot, Han Flat Teapot with colored Glaze, Han Square Teapot with colored Glaze, and so on.

Gold Tracing Decoration

Gold tracing decoration is a costly and complicated process. Fired at a temperature of 750-800 degrees Celsius, the semi-finished product is then painted

• 描金装饰
Gold Tracing Decoration

壶大都由两个人合作完成,一个专门制壶,一个专攻书画,因此通常落款会署上两个名字。字画作者在字画后留铭,壶作者在壶底落款。

描金紫砂壶的特点是壶坯看起来似有颗粒,但手感平滑,摸上去感觉温润细腻;常用竹节形、圆弧形等壶式,壶形优美典雅。但由于工序繁琐,成本很高,因此传世的描金装饰的紫砂壶作品并不多。

镶嵌装饰

镶嵌是一种中国传统的装饰工艺,明清两朝是镶嵌装饰的鼎盛时期。这一时期的紫砂壶运用翡翠、绿松石、青金石、珊瑚、玛瑙、象

again with a special golden liquid in required places. Thereafter, a second firing, with a slightly lower temperature, is performed to produce a finished product. Many of the gold-tracing teapots are jointly worked by two persons, one in charge of making teapots while the other centers on painting decoration. Therefore, both the painter/calligrapher and the teapot maker will inscribe their names on the teapot body, either at the end of the painting or on the bottom of the teapot.

Gold-tracing teapot looks grainy, but feels smooth and warm. It often comes with round shapes or appears as something like a bamboo joint, which looks beautiful and elegant. However, few of these kinds of teapots survived due to the complex and costly process.

Inlay Decoration

Inlay or Tessellation is a traditional decorative method prevalent in the Ming (1368-1644) and Qing (1616-1911) dynasties. Purple clay pot of this period was often decorated with jade, turquoise, lapis lazuli, coral, agate, ivory and other natural materials in a manner of inlaying. The inlaid teapot shows a refined luxury and magnificent decorative effect. In this practice, the clay body is first incised to achieve an intaglio pattern; after firing, various stone materials are filled into the incision. The body is then burnished to reveal the exquisite pattern formed by inlay.

Tessellation decorations on purple clay pot include filigree inlay, slip inlay, glazed pearl inlay, mother-of-pearl inlay, jade inlay, etc. Filigree inlay is to incise down an intaglio pattern on the clay body according to the pre-drawn lines,

• 彩石镶嵌
Stone Inlay

牙等各种天然材质镶嵌，显示出华贵精致、富丽堂皇的装饰效果。其方法是先在紫砂壶坯上刻阴纹，烧成后再嵌入各种镶嵌材料，锉平磨光后，壶身上便展现出由镶嵌形成的精美纹样。

紫砂壶上的镶嵌装饰包括金银丝镶嵌、色泥镶嵌、釉珠镶嵌、螺钿镶嵌、玉石镶嵌等。金银丝镶嵌即先在泥坯上依纹样刻凹线槽，烧成陶后再用金丝、银丝或锡丝敲击嵌入，组成各种装饰图案，线面结合，精美雅观；色泥镶嵌即以壶坯

• 色泥镶嵌
Slip Inlay

本色为底纹，刻出图案，并填、嵌入对比鲜明的包泥，壶烧成后光彩亮丽；釉珠镶嵌一般装饰于紫砂壶的重点突出部位，如龙眼、兽眼及纹样的中心；螺钿、玉石镶嵌源于漆器的装饰方法，即在泥坯上预设镶嵌图案，待壶烧成后髹以黑漆，再在黑漆上将白色螺钿或玉石拼嵌入壶体，突出图案和材质之美。

绞泥装饰

绞泥装饰是运用泥料本身色彩来调配的一种装饰手法，即将两种或多种不同泥料糅合在一起，通过对泥料厚薄的控制和纹扭手法，形成色调对比强烈的不规则线条，从而构成平面视觉效果强烈的装饰图案，如木理纹、花石纹、水波纹、蝴蝶纹、流云纹等，再通过窑烧成

when fired, embed gold, silver or tin wires into the incision to form various decorative patterns; slip inlay is to fill slips of contrasting color into the pre-engraved intaglio patterns on the biscuit body; glazed pearl inlay is generally applied on focused parts of the teapot, such as loong or beast eyes, or center of the patterns; mother-of-pearl and jade inlay is a method derived from lacquer decoration: firstly, draw patterns on the clay body, and then paint black lacquer on the fired teapot; after that, embed white shell powders or jade into the pre-drawn patterns. Teapot made in this way shows a pictorial and material beauty.

Clay Twisting Decoration

Clay twisting decoration is a method using the natural colors of clay materials. It is to blend clays of differing colors but not mix them to the extent that they lose their identities. By adjusting the thickness of clay materials and twisted methods, the wares made have distinctive veined or mottled appearances, like wood grains, water ripples, butterfly patterns, moiré, etc. The colors of clay are of moderate type, and when blended, they give a harmonious note.

- 绞泥装饰
Clay Twisting Decoration

型。紫砂泥的几种泥色都比较含蓄，运用绞泥手法绞在一起显得非常协调。

绞泥工艺起源于唐代，明代时开始运用到紫砂壶的装饰上，到了清代，绞泥装饰已经成为一种成熟的装饰手法。

雕漆装饰

雕漆装饰是紫砂壶特殊装饰技法之一，方法是以紫砂壶为内胎，在紫砂壶表面髹几十道大漆，再用刻刀在漆层上剔刻出繁复精致的花纹图案。传世的雕漆紫砂壶主要是宫廷用品，民间非常少见，因而极为珍贵。

• 雕漆装饰
Carved Lacquer Decoration

The clay twisting method originated in the Tang Dynasty (618-907), was executed decoratively on teapots in the Ming Dynasty (1368-1644) and became a highly developed technique in the Qing Dynasty (1616-1911).

Carved Lacquer Decoration

One of the special decorative techniques, carved lacquer decoration is to encase the biscuit body of the pot in dozens of layers of lacquer. This heavy coating is then carved with complex and delicate patterns. Carved lacquer teapots are very valuable now as they were chiefly made for the royal family and rarely seen outside the imperial court.

Piercing Decoration

Piercing decoration is one of the special decorative techniques applied to purple clay pots. It originated in the late Ming Dynasty and early Qing Dynasty and was prevalent in the regin of Emperor Kangxi, Yongzheng and Qianlong. As the name suggests, piercing is to carve the teapot using hollow cut, and it is further divided into double-layered and single-layered piercing. To be specific, draw on the clay body — either double

镂雕装饰

镂雕装饰是紫砂壶特殊装饰技法之一，始于明末清初，流行于康熙、雍正、乾隆年间。所谓镂雕，即采用镂空技法对紫砂壶进行雕琢，雕刻时又有双层镂雕和单层镂雕之别。其方法是在双层或单层的坯体上，先设计好图案，如人物、山水、书法、诗词等，然后用专用工具，雕出镂空的纹样，使之凸显出来，使壶具有层次感和立体感。

• 镂雕装饰
Piercing Decoration

or single layered — the outline of the patterns inclusive of figures, landscape, calligraphy, poetry, etc., and then perform with special tools the carving on necessary places to raise the patterns or characters to create a three-dimensional effect. This kind of ware is exquisitely made and demands great skills, which leads to its rarity and preciousness.

Tin, Gold, Silver and Copper Encasing Decorations

Tin encasing, formerly applied to jade pots, was borrowed from purple clay pots. It is to encase the teapot in a tin sheet, which is then carved with poetry or painting; the spout, knob and handle, at the same time, are mounted with jade. The finished ware appears elegant and chic. An exquisite decoration, tin encasing comes in many ways — encasing all over the surface of the teapot, encasing the body in the tin while setting the spout, handle and knob in gold, jade or rosewood are among typical examples. However, it was phased out in the reign of Emperor Guangxu (1875-1908) due to the somewhat bulky body that undermines the unique elegance of the teapot.

Very much akin to tin encasing,

镂雕紫砂壶难度高，制作精美，但存世稀少，因此十分珍贵。

包锡、包金银铜装饰

包锡本指锡器包玉壶，后来被紫砂壶借鉴，即在壶外周以锡片包镶，再在锡片上刻画诗文图画，嘴口、盖纽及把均用玉镶接，器成之后高雅别致，是一种有特色的装饰方法。常见的包锡装饰有壶体全包或壶身包锡，壶嘴、壶把或盖纽镶金、玉或红木等。包锡装饰虽外表精致，但略显笨重，并有损紫砂独有的韵味，在清光绪年间就逐渐舍弃不用了。

包金银铜装饰与包锡装饰十分相近，先用透雕纹样的金、银、铜片将壶身包起来，再将壶口和壶盖的边缘也包镶起来，外观非常精美。清代后期，山东威海卫生产包铜紫砂壶，主要出口泰国等东南亚国家。

调砂装饰

在紫砂泥里掺入适量的颗粒状的缸砂（制作缸等大型器物的粗砂），可产生"梨皮""鲨鱼

● 包金装饰
Gold Encasing Decoration

● 包锡装饰
Tin Encasing Decoration

gold, silver and copper encasing are to encase the teapot body in gold, silver or copper sheets with hollow-cut patterns, and then set the rims of spout and lid in these metals. In this way, the teapot shows an extraordinary beauty. Towards the end of the Qing Dynasty, purple clay pot encased in copper was produced in Shandong province for export to Southeast Asian countries.

皮""满天星"等肌理纹样，这种装饰手法被称作"调砂"。具体方法是将处理好的缸砂或紫砂泥矿砂撒置在紫砂泥片的表面，再敲打平整，使砂粒嵌入泥片的表层之内，经烧成后，掺入的砂粒与泥片会形成不同的颜色和肌理效果，增加了紫砂陶的装饰美感。胎土加砂的具体做法有调砂、铺砂两种，都是为了使紫砂壶胎的肌理更加丰富，珠粒隐现，光闪夺目。

Grit Mixing Decoration

Grit Mixing is to mix the purple clay with the right amount of coarse grit, to produce particular textures, like "pear-skin", "shark skin", "stars" and others. The practice goes like this: sprinkle the processed coarse grits on the surface of the clay sheet, and beat the sheet until the grits are embedded in it; when fired, the grits and clay sheet will produce different colors and textures, adding decorative beauty to the teapot. This

- 调砂装饰
  Grit Mixing Decoration

抛光装饰

　　抛光是指在紫砂壶烧成后，用磨料将紫砂壶表面打磨平整，再用抛光剂和毡轮对器表进行抛光处理，产生类似玻璃表面的光泽的装饰技法。抛光紫砂壶的表面光可照人，但紫砂泥原本质朴的肌理不存在了，故在国内并不受欢迎。抛光壶大多为外销壶，主要出口东南亚国家，尤其是泰国。

practice involves grit mixing and grit spreading, all of which will give a richer and dazzling texture to the clay body.

Burnishing Decoration

Burnishing is a process, in which the surface of the fired teapot is burnished by rubbing with suitable materials to produce a glassy finish. Deprived of the pristine texture of the purple clay, this kind of teapot is not popular domestically despite the glassy looks. They are principally intended for export to Southeast Asian countries, Thailand in particular.

- 抛光装饰
  Burnishing Decoration

紫砂壶的包浆

包浆是古玩行业的术语，是器物表面由于空气氧化、土埋水浸、长期的摩挲把玩导致内含物沁出，慢慢形成的覆盖在器物表面的一层化合物。包浆是一种难以伪造的时代特征，传世时间愈久远，包浆也会愈深厚。对于紫砂壶来说，包浆不但能使壶体看上去更加古雅，具有一种自然含蓄、温润如玉的光泽，而且宜茶性也会更好。

Baojiang of Teapot

Baojiang is a terminology used in the antique industry. It is a special coating formed by something oozed slowly onto the surface of the ware due to air oxidation, prolonged touching, burying in the earth or water soaking. This coating admirably brings a natural, subtle and warm luster to the teapot, giving it a note of classic elegance, and is more suitable for tea steeping.

- 已形成包浆的紫砂壶
  Purple Clay Pot with *Baojiang*

> 紫砂壶的款识

款识是紫砂壶制作中一种特殊的工艺，是将用来表明年代、人名、堂名，或者表示赞颂、祝愿等内容的文字，印刻在器物的底部或其他部位。据文献记载，从供春壶开始，紫砂壶就已有款识了。历代紫砂制壶大师对款识都十分讲究，款识已成为彰显制壶者文化艺术素养的方式，融入了很多书法篆刻的手法。紫砂壶的款识发展经历了由刻款到印款的工艺演变过程，虽为紫砂壶的附属物，但可与其他装饰配合，增强器物的艺术性。

刻款

刻款即将款识刻在壶体上，工艺与刻画装饰相似。从传世的紫砂壶上看，最早的紫砂壶款识，即供

> Inscriptions of Purple Clay Pot

The inscription is a special craft used to indicate age, names, or text expressing wishes or tributes, which is engraved on the bottom or elsewhere of the teapot. According to records, the inscriptions appeared very early in history. It reflects the cultural awareness of producers. Masters in various dynasties attached great importance to it, and also integrated numerous techniques of calligraphy and seal carving into the inscriptions. An appendage though, it is able to bring more artistic flavor to the teapot together with other decorations. In its development, the inscriptions evolved gradually from engraving to seal carving.

Engraving Inscriptions

Engraving is to carve the inscriptions on the teapot body, similar to carving

刻款
Engraving Inscriptions

春制壶，便是刻款。

　　紫砂壶上的刻款一般是在制壶坯时用竹刀或钢刀刻上去的，在刀法上要充分体现刀在紫砂壶泥坯上的刻划之痕，追求明快质朴，运刀流畅。经过烧制，笔画刀口会形成结晶光面。

　　刻款要求制壶艺人具有一定的书法基础，而早期的紫砂工匠并不精于此，只得请人落墨镌款，因此就出现了专门的"工镌壶款"之人。明代刻款非常流行，时大彬最早的款识便是请人用毛笔预先题写在紫砂坯体上，然后自己用竹刀在坯体上依毛笔的提顿转折逐笔刻划。后来随着技艺的熟练，时大彬不再请人落墨，而是以刀代笔直接

decorations. Among the extant pieces, the oldest surviving inscriptions were in the manner of engraving found on teapots by Gong Chun.

　　A bamboo knife or steel knife is normally used to carve the inscriptions on the clay body. The cutting technique is required to be quick, simple and smooth to fully demonstrate the beautiful cutting marks. When fired, the edges of the cutting marks appear smooth and crystal clear.

　　The engraving of inscriptions requires the artisans to be somewhat proficient in calligraphy, while early artisans, not familiar with this, had to obtain the services of other writers — the experts on carving this sort of thing — to do so. This practice was very popular in the

刻画，形成了后人难以模仿的个人风格。

由于刻款工艺复杂，至清代逐渐被印款取代，刻款只用于刻铭文，大部分用行书或篆书，也有少数使用楷书。

印款

印款即将款识印在壶体上，一般为一人独立完成。

印款与刻款相比具有许多优势：首先，如果艺人不擅长书法，可以请人刻一方印，然后自己便可重复使用；其次，在壶上用印，方便易行，比在壶上刻款更加便捷，适用于批量生产。因此在清代初期，印款开始普及，并取代了刻款。但也有一些制壶名家书法较好，刻款与印款并用。

印款的形式很丰富，有圆形、半圆形、椭圆形、长方形、正方形、葫芦形、瓦当形、自然形和肖形等形状；款识字体有楷书、小篆、缪篆、隶书等；款识的内容除制壶艺人的姓名外，也可表示定制者、监制者、纪年，还有斋名、堂名、馆名、室名、工厂和商号名

Ming Dynasty (1368-1644). In his early period, Shi Dabin, the celebrated teapot artisan, needed the help of a scholar to inscribe the pot, and then he carved along the written strokes with a bamboo knife. Later, with the improvement of the skills, Shi carved directly on the clay body and formed his unique style.

Because of its complexity, engraving of inscriptions was gradually replaced by seal inscription in the Qing Dynasty (1616-1911), except for a few cases of epigraph in running script or seal script applied on teapots.

Seal Inscriptions

Seal Inscription is to stamp the seal on the body of the teapot, and is often completed independently by the artisans.

Seal is in many ways superior to engraving: first of all, artisans who are not good at calligraphy may have a seal made for repeated use; second, it is easier to seal the inscriptions on the teapot body than to engrave, and this is applicable to mass production. For this reason, seal inscriptions became overwhelmingly dominant in the early Qing Dynasty. Nevertheless, engraving was still active among some artisans accomplished in

称，以及寓意吉祥的图案。

紫砂壶上的印款跟书画作品上的印章一样，首先要大小适中，与壶的大小相匹配；其次要位置得当，一般应钤在壶的底部、盖内、鋬下，尤其是用在明处时，更要审察位置是否合适；三要讲究布局匀称、呼应和谐；四要求印款的内容与壶形风格协调；五要讲究钤印的轻重适宜，要恰到好处地体现出印文的金石风格。

calligraphy.

There are a great variety of seal inscriptions, like circular, semicircular, ellipse, rectangular, square, gourd shape, tile shape, natural shape, animal shape, etc., the character style featuring regular script, seal script, official script and others. Aside from artisan's name, seal inscriptions are also used to indicate age, the names of commissioners, executive producers, studios, factories and firms, as well as auspicious patterns.

Similar to those on paintings or calligraphic works, seal inscriptions on the teapot are required to be moderate in size to match the teapot body; also, the inscriptions should be placed where appropriate — on the bottom, inside the lid, on the handle or elsewhere. Further, the layout is required to be reasonable and harmonious, and the content of the inscriptions is to be compatible with the shape of the teapot. Lastly, stamp the seal with appropriate force so that the seal mark perfectly reflects the epigraphic style of the inscriptions.

- 印款
  Seal Inscriptions

赏壶四字诀

鉴赏一把紫砂壶，要从四个方面入手——"形""神""气""态"，即紫砂壶的造型、外观、色泽、品相、气质等自身特征的概括。

（1）形，即看外观造型。不论什么形状的紫砂壶，都要给人以协调舒服的感觉。

（2）神，即看质地。不管是哪种泥色的紫砂壶，都一定要温润。这种温润应该是自然的，与生俱来的。

（3）气，即看功能。要注意壶嘴出水是否流畅，壶盖是否紧密等。传世的紫砂壶精品，将壶盖盖上后，提着盖纽便能将整把壶都拎起来。可惜这种高水平的技艺，如今很少见了。

（4）态，即看装饰。一把好的紫砂壶，不但要求形态美，还要求形神兼备，即外在的装饰要与壶的形体相协调。

• 紫砂壶精品
Purple Clay Pot Masterworks

Four Tips on Appreciation of Teapot

The appreciation of purple clay pot involves these aspects — shape, appearance, color, texture, condition and so on.

1. Any teapot, no matter what shapes, should have a comfortable feeling.

2. The texture of a teapot, regardless of color, is to be warm and moist naturally and innately.

3. The spout should pass water smoothly; the lid and the opening should meet seamlessly. For some teapot masterworks, one will be able to lift a lidded teapot by simply holding the knob with fingers. Unfortunately, such a superior skill is rarely seen today.

4. A good teapot requires not only beautiful shape but also exquisite decorations in harmony with the shape.

妙手壶家
Masters of Teapot

自紫砂壶诞生以来，涌现出众多艺术大师。他们通过对紫砂壶的精心制作，张扬着自己的个性。也正因为一代又一代紫砂艺人的不断努力，才造就了今天精美绝伦的紫砂壶艺术品。

A great many masters have emerged since the purple clay pot was born. It was their elaboration, unique personality, and unremitting efforts that created the teapot masterworks of today.

> 供春

供春（明正德、嘉靖年间），有紫砂壶作品传世第一人的美誉。据史料记载，供春本是宜兴吴氏的一名家僮，侍候主人在金沙寺中读书，而后跟随金沙寺僧学习制壶技

> Gong Chun

The earliest purple-clay artist recorded was Gong Chun of the Ming Dynasty. He was a boy servant to Wu Yishan, a native of Yixing. Wu spent some time in Jinsha temple, preparing himself for the imperial examination. On these occasions, he brought Gong Chun with him to attend to his chores. Gong Chun, when his services were not needed, would apprentice to an old monk — said to have been the initiator of purple clay pot — in this temple. The first teapot made by Gong Chun was so much favored by his master that he had several copies of this teapot made by Gong Chun and invited

- 树瘿壶（供春制）

树瘿壶外形似银杏树的树瘿，壶的把梢旁有"供春"二字刻款；壶身为不规则扁球形，壶嘴及壶把与壶身浑然一体，均呈栗色，有似老松树皮的肌理；壶把于中段分支作松根状，壶身轻巧，端握舒适。壶的整体造型古拙，有天然妙成之趣。

Gall Teapot by Cong Chun

This teapot looks like the galls of a ginko tree. At the end of the handle are carved two characters "供春" (Gong Chun); the body appears as an irregular oblate sphere; the lid and the handle as well as the body are blended into a harmonious whole, all presenting a chestnut color and resembling the bark of an old pine tree; the handle bifurcates midway to shape like the root of pine tree. The teapot is very light and feels right in the hand. Boasting of primitive and simple appearance, it is exactly like a gift of God.

艺。有一次，供春所制之壶偶然被主人吴氏看到，该壶质朴古雅，十分精致。吴氏便叫他照样再做几把，并且请当时名流来鉴赏。名流们见壶后，齐声叫好，从此供春壶名声大噪。

相传供春最初捏制紫砂壶时，所用的陶土非同一般。他选用的泥特别纯净、细腻，杂质甚少，胎体甚薄，因此造出的紫砂壶十分轻巧。

供春所制紫砂壶受时人所爱，收藏家竞相收购，有所谓"供春之壶，胜于金玉"之说。除树瘿壶外，供春还创制了"龙蛋""刻角印方"等壶，但已失传。

celebrities to view them. These were very much appreciated, and teapots by Gong Chun had since become popular.

It is said that early teapot works of Gong Chun were made of extremely pure and fine clay with very few impurities. The clay body featured extraordinarily thin walls, and the fired teapots were very light.

The teapots by Gong Chun were hailed as "more precious than gold and jade", and were highly prized by tea drinkers and collectors of the time. Apart from the Gall Teapot, his famous works also included"The Loong Egg Teapot", "Square Teapot with Four Feet" and others, but none of them survived.

千人仿一壶

供春所创制的树瘿壶是他唯一的存世之作，也是被仿制得最多的一件作品。相传当时供春无意中看到金沙寺旁一棵大银杏树的树瘿，随即仿照树瘤的形状制了一把壶，并刻上树瘿上的花纹。供春平日结交了一些文人墨客，大家常在一起饮茶、谈论文学。这些文人见到这把树瘿壶，觉得十分古朴可爱，于是竞相仿制。由于树瘿壶在紫砂历史上的特殊地位，几乎历代所有的知名紫砂艺人都仿制过它，且出了不少精品，因此有"千人仿一壶"之说。

A Teapot with Thousands of Copies

The Gall Teapot is Gong Chun's only surviving piece and has been copied oftentimes. It is said that Gong Chun, inspired by the galls of the ginko tree near the Jinsha Temple, had made the teapot and carved on the teapot body the patterns of the galls. Gong Chun and his friends —

usually consisting of literati and scholars — often held parties drinking tea or engaging in literary discussions. These were so fond of the gall teapot that they thronged to copy it. Because of its particular status in the history of purple clay ware, this teapot had been modeled after by almost all celebrated artisans of various dynasties, which contributed to numerous masterworks, and this is the legend of "a Teapot with thousands of copies".

- 仿供春树瘿壶（黄玉麟制）
Gall Teapot by Huang Yulin Modeled after the Teapot by Gong Chun

- 仿供春树瘿壶（邵陆大制）
Gall Teapot by Shao Luda Modeled after the Teapot by Gong Chun

- 仿供春树瘿壶（徐秀棠制）
Gall Teapot by Xu Xiutang Modeled after the Teapot by Gong Chun

> 时大彬

时大彬（1573—1648），明代制壶名家，是继供春之后，知名度最高、影响力最深的一位壶艺大家。时大彬乃是宜兴制陶名艺人时朋之子，自小跟从其父学习制壶技艺，到万历后期已享誉艺林，所制"大彬壶"受到各阶层爱茶人士和收藏家的追捧。

时大彬对紫砂壶艺的贡献主要体现在制作工艺、配泥、造型、艺

> Shi Dabin (1573-1648)

Shi Dabin of the Ming Dynasty was the most famous and influential teapot artist after Gong Chun. Son of a celebrated potter, Shi Peng of Yixing, Dabin apprenticed to his father from very early on, and made a name for himself in the late Wanli period. Teapots made by Shi were much sought after by tea drinkers and collectors of various classes.

The contributions Shi Dabin made to purple clay pots are chiefly represented in these areas — potting skills, mixing of

壶盖：壶盖及壶口部分做成六瓣肥厚的花托，与花瓣组成的大壶体形成叠压和对比关系。

Lid: the lid and the opening, acting as the full and rounded receptacle, provide an arresting contrast with the big body composed of flower petals.

壶身：六个花瓣、花托的曲率线形工整一致，形成了强烈的照应关系。

Body: the six petals and the receptacle are of the same curvature, appearing harmonized and well-balanced.

- 紫砂玉兰花六瓣壶（时大彬制）

此壶以一朵六瓣玉兰花为壶形，壶盖是玉兰花蒂，流和壶把都是曲线形，与玉兰壶体十分融洽，壶底部刻款为"万历丁酉春时大彬制"。

Magnolia Petal Teapot, by Shi Dabin

This teapot is in the shape of an upturned magnolia flower, and the lid is the flower pedicle; the spout and the handle are curved merging with the flower-like body. "万历丁酉春时大彬制" (made by Shi Dabin in the spring of 1597).

- **龙带壶（时大彬制）**

此壶以龙带为饰，龙带自壶口四周肩部由上而下地向左右两边展开，线面清晰。壶底刻有"大彬仿供春式"六字楷书款。整壶造型简练大方、古朴雅致。

Loong Belt Teapot, by Shi Dabin

As the decoration of this teapot, the loong belt is slightly raised up from the teapot body and is expanded to the left and the right down from the shoulder. On the bottom of the teapot are carved six characters in regular script which read "大彬仿供春式" (teapot made by Shi Dabin modeled after the one by Gong Chun). The teapot looks simple yet elegant.

- **如意纹盖三足壶（时大彬制）**

此壶浑圆而扁，下承三钝锥形矮足，壶肩部以上竖立一圈短颈，颈上置一压盖，壶盖四周贴有柿蒂如意纹，盖纽如珠，中部留有出气孔。

Three-foot Teapot with a Lid Carved with *Ruyi* Patterns, by Shi Dabin

This teapot is of oblate shape and rests on three cone-shaped short legs. Over the shoulder is a short neck, covered by a lid. The lid is decorated with *Ruyi* patterns in the manner of appliqué. In the center of the pearl-like knob, there is a vent hole.

术风格以及识款题铭五个方面。首先，在制作工艺上，时大彬确立了手工成型的制壶技术；其次，在配泥上，时大彬首次在制壶泥料中掺入细小的生泥粒子，发明"调砂"工艺，开创了调砂法制壶。除了调砂外，时大彬还首创了通过调配泥色来增强紫砂壶美感的方法；第三，在造型上，时大彬改大壶为小壶，开创了方形、圆形、仿生象形器及筋囊器等多种经典壶式；第四，在艺术风格上，时大彬形成了

clay materials, shaping, artistic style and inscriptions on the teapot. First of all, Shi established the potting skills of manually shaping. Secondly, he founded a new way of teapot making, that is, mixing fine raw clay particles with clay materials; besides, he was also the first one to enhance the beauty of purple clay pot by deftly mixing the colors of clay materials. Thirdly, Shi reduced the size of the teapots and set up various new shapes, like square, round, veined as well as those in the shape of animals and plants.

自己敦雅古穆的独特风格；第五，在识款题铭上，时大彬在紫砂壶的刻款上表现出很高的文化修养，将书法与留款结合起来，并开创了壶上题铭的先河。

紫砂壶艺到时大彬时已基本发展成熟，加上他广纳门徒，传技授艺，使得紫砂壶艺术在他手中发扬光大，蔚为大观。

> 惠孟臣

惠孟臣（约明代天启到清代康熙年间），壶艺名家。惠孟臣壶艺出众，所制壶式有高身、梨形、鼓腹、折腹、平肩等，以小壶多，中壶少，大壶最少。后期专做朱砂小壶，造型奇，体积小，工艺精，每把壶都修饰得光泽莹润，线条圆转流畅，成为其突出的风格特征。这

Fourthly, he formed his unique style, which was simple, solemn and elegant. Last but not least, with inscriptions and calligraphy combined, the inscriptions he made were of highly cultural refinement, setting a precedent for teapot inscriptions.

The skills of teapot making were matured in Shi's period, and they were further improved and flourished owing to Shi and his disciples.

> Hui Mengchen

Hui Mengchen was a distinguished teapot artist in late Ming Dynasty, and he was particularly known for his outstanding potting skills. His works are of a few varieties of shapes — high stature, pear shape, bulging belly or broken-line belly, flat shoulder, etc., and are mostly small-sized. In his later years, Hui centered on nothing but small teapots, which were characterized by their unique shape, compactness and superior craftsmanship. Each of these teapots shows mellow

- 包金朱泥壶（惠孟臣制）
此壶选用朱泥制成，胎质细薄，壶身为滚圆的球形，小巧玲珑，雅致脱俗。
Zhuni Teapot Set in Gold, by Hui Mengchen.
Made of *Zhuni* (cinnabar clay), this teapot has a fine and thin clay body. It is of spherical shape, small and exquisite, elegant and refined.

- **矮梨式壶（惠孟臣制）**

矮梨式壶是惠孟臣所制小壶中的一种。壶身似矮梨，截盖，珠形纽，耳形壶把，一捺底。

Teapot in Shape of Squat Pear, by Hui Mengchen

This teapot is one of those small pieces produced by Hui Mengchen. The body appears as a squat pear, the lid is of the truncated type. The pot has an ear-shaped handle and a flat base.

种壶被誉为"孟臣壶"，在闽粤地区备受欢迎。孟臣壶在同时期和后世都多有仿制。此外，惠孟臣还擅配制多种调砂泥，以朱紫者多，白砂者少。孟臣壶署款在壶底以竹刀镌刻，皆为行书。

> 陈鸣远

陈鸣远（清康熙年间），清初最有名的紫砂巨匠。陈鸣远生于紫砂世家，技艺精湛全面，所制花货、光货、筋囊货、文玩摆件均精

luster and smooth curves, highlighting Hui's hallmark. Hailed as "Mengchen Teapot", these pieces were much sought after in Fujian and Guangdong provinces. Hui's teapot was copied both in his day and in later period. In addition, Hui was also good at mixing clay materials, most of which came with cinnabar and purple color, and few with white. The inscriptions of Mengchen teapot were found carved at the bottom of the teapot with bamboo knife, in running script.

> Chen Mingyuan

Born in a family of potters, Chen Mingyuan was active during the reign of Emperor Kangxi (1662-1722). He was the most eminent teapot artist in the early Qing Dynasty and had masterful and comprehensive skills. Although Chen was known to all for his sculpture pot, smooth pot, veined pot and small antiques, he was particularly remarkable for his sculpture pieces. His works was exquisite and of superlative craftsmanship. Melon-shaped Teapot, Lotus Seed Teapot, Firewood Bundle Teapot, Pine Tree Teapot, Plum Tree Teapot, Silkworm and Mulberry Teapot are among the extant pieces. These pots enjoy vivid and lively

● 松段壶（陈鸣远制）

此壶仿松树老干之形，松树干苍老的形态、松树皮的肌理都做得惟妙惟肖；壶盖采用嵌入式，使壶形保持了松树段之形；底刻款"鸣远"，印款"陈鸣远"。

Pine Tree Teapot, by Chen Mingyuan

This teapot is modeled after an old pine tree trunk, the appearance of the trunk and the texture of the bark are very realistic; the lid is sunk into the lip of the opening to better keep the shape of the tree trunk; on the base is engraved "鸣远" (Mingyuan) and stamped a seal "陈鸣远" (Chen Mingyuan).

提梁：提梁采用软提梁结构，为一根形作藕节的银质弧形提梁。

Upper Handle: the movable upper handle of this teapot resembles an arc-shaped lotus root and is made of silver.

壶嘴：塑卷荷叶为直流。

Spout: the straight spout appears as a furled lotus leaf.

壶盖：壶盖采用嵌入式，作莲蓬形，盖面上一周嵌有六颗可活动的莲子，中部是可转动的珠形纽。

Lid: the lid is in the shape of lotus seed pod and is of embedded type. On the lid a turnable pearl-like knob is surrounded by six movable lotus seed.

铭文：在壶外壁的莲瓣上刻有行楷铭文。

Inscription: on one of the lotus petals is engraved the inscription in Xingkai script (A type of running script, similar to but not as much rigid as the regular script.).

壶身：此壶塑八瓣莲花围绕一莲蓬造型为壶体。

Body: the body is composed of eight petals around a seedpod.

● 莲形银佩壶（陈鸣远制）

Lotus Teapot, by Chen Mingyuan

• 菱花式壶（陈鸣远制）

此壶以菱花花瓣为造型，纹络清晰端正，做工十分精细。

Teapot in Shape of Water Chestnut Flower, by Chen Mingyuan

This teapot is of superb craftsmanship. The body is designed to shape like the petals of water chestnut flower, and the veins are overt and upright.

雅俏丽，鬼斧神工，尤以擅制花货著称，传世品有瓜形壶、莲子壶、束柴三友壶、松段壶、梅干壶、蚕桑壶等，极具自然生趣，将自然型壶推向了艺术的高峰。

陈鸣远制壶讲究自然天趣，并开创了壶体镌刻诗铭之风，提高了紫砂壶的艺术价值和文化价值。壶上署款时刻名和印章并用，款式健雅。因处盛世，陈鸣远所制壶难免受清代乾隆时期奢靡之风的影响，有繁缛靡弱之态。

appearances, elevating the sculpture teapots to a higher artistic level.

Chen Mingyuan laid special emphasis on making articles to simulate nature, and he was keen on engraving inscriptions on teapots, which enhanced the artistic and cultural value of purple clay pots. On his teapots he applied both engraving and seal stamping of vigorous and elegant designs. Living in the most prosperous era of the Qing Dynasty, Chen's works owed much to the extravagant, over-elaborate and decadent style prevalent in this period.

> The Yang Family

The Yang family, namely, teapot artisans Yang Pengnian, Yang Baonian and Yang Fengnian, were active during the reign of Emperor Qianlong and Jiaqing. All three were eminent artists, whose works featured simple, elegant and exquisite shapes. By jointly working with literati and then closely associating purple clay pots with them, the Yang family made great contributions to the art of purple clay pot, and the cultural value and artistic quality of teapots were therefore lifted to a high level. The Yang family, cooperating with such literati as Chen

> 杨氏兄妹

杨氏兄妹（清乾隆、嘉庆年间），即制壶名家杨彭年、杨宝年、杨凤年三兄妹。杨氏兄妹擅制紫砂壶，所制壶造型浑朴雅致，精巧玲珑。杨氏兄妹对紫砂壶艺的最大贡献在于与文人合作制壶，将紫

Mansheng, produced a great number of top-class purple clay wares.

Of the three, Yang Pengnian was credited with the highest achievements. He was skillful at mixing clay materials and engraving bamboos. By deftly using the kneading technique formerly adopted by Shi Dabin, his work was naturally grown. When making teapot, Pengnian

- **箬笠壶（杨彭年制 陈曼生铭）**
此壶形似箬笠，造型简朴，色泽古雅。斗笠是中国古代的农民使用的头戴式遮阳遮雨用具，也是隐居乡村的文人常用之物。陈曼生在壶身上刻有铭文"笠荫暍，茶去渴，是二是一，我佛无说"，意思是：斗笠能遮阴，饮茶能解渴，这两种去暑的方式是一回事，还是两回事，佛祖没有明示。

Bamboo Hat Teapot, made by Yang Pengnian, inscribed by Chen Mansheng
Modeled after a bamboo hat, this teapot is of simple shape and quaint luster. Bamboo hat is the appliance that ancient Chinese farmers used for sunshade or rain-proof purposes, and is also commonly used by reclusive scholars. On the teapot body there is an inscription by Chen Mansheng that reads "Bamboo hat is able to keep out the sun, while tea can quench thirst, and Buddha does not express whether or not these two are the same."

- **直腹刻铭曼生壶（杨彭年制）**
此壶造型小巧可爱，壶身扁圆，宽斜肩，直腹，下腹斜收，耳形壶把，壶盖为平顶压盖式，桥形纽。

Flat Belly Mansheng Teapot with Inscriptions, by Yang Pengnian
This small and cute teapot features an oblate spherical body, wide oblique shoulder and flat belly. The lower part of the belly is tapered to the base. The handle is of ear shape, the lid with a flat top covers on the opening, and in the center of the lid there is a knob in the shape of bridge.

砂壶与中国文人紧密联系在一起，使得紫砂壶的文化价值和艺术品位得到提升。他们与陈曼生等文人合作，制作了一大批高品质的紫砂器。

三兄妹中，杨彭年制壶的成就最高。杨彭年擅配泥色，兼擅刻竹，沿袭了时大彬的捏造法，作品充满天然之趣。杨彭年制壶无需用

required no mold, he kneaded the mixed clay freely with his hands, and there was not even the slightest trace of adhesion on the teapot, especially the spout, although it was assembled in the manner of attaching, it was blended into the body as a harmonious whole. The teapots of various shapes seemed natural and delicate.

- 飞鸿延年壶（杨彭年制）

此壶是曼生壶式的一种，腹部饱满，一面刻隶书"延年壶"，另一面刻行书若干字，署"曼生为止侯铭"款。

Feihong Yannian Teapot, by Yang Pengnian

This piece belongs to the Mansheng-style teapots. It has a full and plump belly, on one side of which is engraved in official script "延年壶" (*Yannian* Teapot), on the other side are engraved several characters in running script, with a signature that read "曼生为止侯铭" (Dedicated to Zhihou by Mansheng).

- 风卷葵壶（杨凤年制）

Sunflower Teapot, by Yang Fengnian

- 竹段壶（杨凤年制）

Bamboo Teapot, by Yang Fengnian

模子复制，只用一双手，将配好的泥随意捏造，看不到任何粘连的痕迹，尤其是壶嘴，虽然是粘上去的，但看上去与壶身浑然一体，各种形状的紫砂壶似乎是天然生成，十分精巧。

> 邵大亨

邵大亨（清道光、咸丰年间），清代制壶大家，所制壶有"一壶千金，几不可得"之誉。邵大亨技艺卓越，秉性刚烈，情趣闲

- **鱼化龙壶（邵大亨制）**
圆形的壶体作海水波浪图案；壶盖波涛涌起，立体雕出龙首探出，且伸缩自如；壶柄作龙尾，如蛟龙浮海，神气活现。
Fish-transfigured-into-loong Teapot, by Shao Daheng
This round teapot has water wave patterns on the body; the lid looks like surging waves, with a movable loong head on the top; the handle is designed to be the loong tail, just like a mighty loong floating on the sea.

> Shao Daheng

Shao Daheng was a renowned teapot artist active during the reign of Emperor Daoguang and Xianfeng, and his works were hailed as "more precious than gold." Shao, accomplished in potting skills, was said to have staunch character and leisurely taste. He gained fame at a very early age and was another master after Chen Mingyuan.

Shao made a great impact on the style of purple clay pot of the Qing Dynasty (1616-1911). He resumed the primitive simplicity and elegance by getting rid of the over-elaborate and somewhat decadent style during the prosperous era of the Qing Dynasty, improving the artistic style of the teapot. He was adept at making simple and unadorned teapots, particularly such pieces as Ball Teapots, Archaized Teapots, etc. These teapots featured a simple, solemn and imposing style, highlighting the rustic and elegant style of the art of purple clay pot. Gu Jingzhou, the master of Chinese industrial art spoke highly of him, "The survived teapots by Shao were undisputed masterpieces, which completely changed the ornate and decadent style. His preparation of the

- 德钟壶（邵大亨制）

  此壶大口唇边，短颈，圆棱四方形，直流前伸，耳形壶把，器形十分端庄，壶呈色紫润，系用天然泥色制成。壶盖内有"大亨"楷书印款。

  Dezhong Teapot, by Shao Daheng

  This teapot features a large opening circled with a plain rim on the outside; under the short neck is the body, and the edges of the body are not angular but slightly curved; on the opposite of the straight spout is an ear-shaped handle. This piece, made of mellow purplish clay, is of very dignified shape. Inside the lid is stamped a seal "大亨" (Daheng) in regular script.

- 仿古壶（邵大亨制）

  Archaized Teapot, by Shao Daheng

逸，少年时便享有盛名，是继陈鸣远之后的一代宗师。

邵大亨对于清代紫砂壶风格的发展影响极大，他一改紫砂艺术在盛清阶段的繁缛靡弱之态，使其重新回归质朴典雅，提高了紫砂壶的格调。他制壶以浑朴见长，尤喜制简练器形如掇球、仿古等壶，朴实庄重，气势不凡，突出紫砂艺术质朴典雅的风格。中国工艺美术大师顾景舟曾评价他："（邵大亨）的各式传器，堪称集砂艺大成，刷一代纤巧糜

clay material, his unique aesthetic touch, his superb techniques, were much praised by all, his reputation was too high not to be unprecedented."

In addition, Shao's teapots were represented by complete form, practical functions and superior skills. His extant works are exemplified by Ball Teapot, Fish-transfigured-into-loong Teapot, Sunflower Teapot, Bamboo Bundle Teapot and others.

> ## Huang Yulin

Huang Yulin was a distinguished teapot

繁之风。从他选泥的精练，造型上审美之奥邃，创作形式上的完美，技艺的高超，博得一时传颂，盛誉之高，大有'前不见古人，后不见来者'之慨。"

此外，邵大亨的壶既讲究形式上的完整、功能上的适用，又讲究精深的表现技巧，传世作品有掇球壶、鱼化龙壶、风卷葵壶、束竹八卦壶等。

> 黄玉麟

黄玉麟（清末），宜兴著名的制壶大家。黄玉麟13岁时便开始学习制壶技艺，擅制掇球、供春、鱼

artist active in the late Qing Dynasty. He began learning potting craft at the age of 13, and he was skillful at making teapots in such styles as Ball, Gong Chun, Fish-transfigured-into-loong, etc. His works were fitted with beautiful curves and loveliness, showing an exquisite note and an air of antiquity.

Huang was once invited to make teapots by some officials at their homes. One of the officials, Wu Dacheng, was a well-known collector who had a large number of ancient bronze wares and pottery. Inspired by these ancient pieces, Huang digested many features from them to further improve his potting skills, leaving behind a lot of excellent works.

Adept at mixing clay materials,

● **方斗壶（黄玉麟制）**
此壶因以量米的方斗为壶式而得名。壶身为四棱台形，直流和壶把都做成方形，安装在方斗形壶身相对的两个面上。壶盖采用嵌盖式，盖纽为方柱体。盖内印款为"玉麟"。

Square *Dou* Teapot, by Huang Yulin
As the name suggests, this teapot is of the shape of a square measure used to hold rice. The body looks like a pyramid with the peak truncated, both the spout and the handle are of square in section, looking at each other across the square opening; the lid is sunk into the lip of the opening, and is surmounted with a cubic knob. Inside the lid is stamped a seal "玉麟" (Yulin).

化龙等壶式，作品圆润可爱，精巧而不失古意。

黄玉麟曾先后受朝廷官员吴大澂和顾茶林之邀，为他们制壶。吴大澂是金石收藏家，黄玉麟在吴家时看到了许多古代的铜器和陶器，他把这些古器物的艺术特色融入到紫砂壶的创作中，使他的壶艺更加精进，给后人留下了许多佳作。

此外，黄玉麟还擅配泥料，所制茗壶选泥十分讲究，晚年每制一壶，必精心构撰。除了紫砂壶，他还擅长创制紫砂工艺假山盆景。

Huang gave great attention to choosing the materials used for each teapot. In his later years, each of his teapots had elaborate designs and was time-consuming. Though marked with a very high price, the teapots were much sought after by collectors. Besides teapots, he was accomplished in making rockery bonsais with purple clay craft.

- 鱼化龙壶（黄玉麟制）

  黄玉麟所制的鱼化龙壶，壶面云浪纹，舒展流畅；鱼、龙、云浮雕装饰与壶身浑然一体，刻画精细，整体呈现奇巧俏丽的风格。

  Fish-transfigured-into-loong Teapot, by Huang Yulin

  This teapot has smooth and stretching water wave patterns on the body; the fish, loong and cloud patterns are exquisitely done by way of bas-relief, and are integrated seamlessly into the body, lending a unique and slender beauty to the teapot.

> 程寿珍

程寿珍，清末民初的紫砂壶名家。程寿珍是清代著名制壶艺人邵友廷的养子，自幼随父学艺，基础扎实，技艺纯熟，作品形制朴素，粗犷中别有韵味，擅长制作掇球壶等仿古壶式。程寿珍一生勤劳多产，年过七十尚制作不辍，一生所制紫砂壶不计其数，流传民间甚多。

程寿珍中晚年仅制掇球、仿鼓、汉扁三种壶式，钤印有"冰心道人""八十二老人"等。其中，掇球壶曾于1915年在巴拿马万国博览会及1932年在美国芝加哥博览会

• 掇球壶（程寿珍制）
Ball Teapot, by Cheng Shouzhen

> Cheng Shouzhen

Cheng Shouzhen, an eminent teapot artist active in the late Qing Dynasty, was the adoptive son of Shao Youting — another celebrated teapot artist. Cheng became apprenticed to his adoptive father very early on and therefore developed superior skills. His works are of simple shapes, rustic but appealing. He was an expert on making archaized pieces, like the Ball Teapot. Owing to his long career, Chen was a prolific artist. Many of his countless works are extant today.

In his remaining years, Cheng focused exclusively on these styles — the Ball Teapot, Drum-shaped Teapot and Han Flat Teapot, the seals of "冰心道人" (Pure-hearted Taoist) or "八十二老人" (82-year-old Man) being often stamped on his works. Of his pieces, the Ball Teapot won prizes at the Panama Pacific International Exposition in 1915 and the Chicago Exposition in 1932 respectively, thus became very famous at the time. Since then, he has included the following inscription and seals in all copies of Ball Teapot — on the base is carved an inscription that reads "This teapot is made by an 82-year-old, and won prize in Panama Pacific International Exposition",

- **汉扁壶（程寿珍制）**

汉扁壶是仿汉代青铜扁壶而成的紫砂壶式。此壶古朴素雅，底印有"冰心道人"款。

Han Flat Teapot, by Cheng Shouzhen

This kind of teapot is modeled on the squat bronze pot of the Han Dynasty (206B.C.—220A.D.). The piece appears simple and elegant, and on the base is stamped the seal "冰心道人" (Pure-hearted Taoist).

获奖，名重一时。此后，其所制掇球壶，便底钤有"八十二老人作此茗壶，巴拿马和国货物品展览会曾得优奖"款识，盖印篆书"寿珍"印，并有"真记"楷书小印。

> 俞国良

俞国良（1874—1939），清末民初的著名紫砂壶艺人、陶瓷艺人。俞国良的紫砂壶作品精工和技巧兼备，擅制仿古品。俞国良技艺出众，声名远播，但大半生都漂泊在外，生活并不如意。他曾到苏州吴大澂家中制壶，用印"斋"，所做壶式有汉君壶、乳鼎壶、白泥大

on the lid of which is stamped the seal "寿珍" (Shouzhen) in seal script, on the handle a tiny seal "真记" (Authentic Product) in regular script.

> Yu Guoliang (1874-1939)

Yu Guoliang was a well-known ceramic artist active in the late nineteenth century and early twentieth century. He was adept in making archaized wares, and his purple clay pots are exemplified by superior craftsmanship and skills. Although Yu enjoyed great potting skills and a high reputation, this did not bring him wealth — he led a wandering life in almost half of his days. He was once invited by Wu Dacheng of Suzhou to

- 提梁壶（俞国良制）

此壶不仅泥料罕见，表面呈冷白色，而且造型别致，做工精细。壶身形状特别，似石础更似柱础，壶底与壶身衔接处弧线挺括有力；平肩嵌盖桥钮，刚柔并济。最有特点的是提梁，靠壶嘴的方向成枝杈形状，三叉交点下移并略向内凹，含蓄秀美，是提梁壶中不可多得的精品。

Upper Handle Teapot, by Yu Guoliang

This teapot, made of rare white clay, is of unique style and fine workmanship. The body looks like a stone plinth, the curves linking the base and the body are firm and smooth; the flat shoulder, the bridge-shaped knob and the embedded lid integrate hardness with softness; the upper handle is the focus of this teapot—it bifurcates near the spout, the intersection is designed to be moved down a little and to slightly recess inwards. The subtle balance and elegance make this teapot a wonderful work of art.

- 红大传炉壶（俞国良制）

此壶精选最好的大红泥制作，朱红泽润，光彩照人，盖铃印"国良"。

Big Red Furnace Teapot, by Yu Guoliang

This teapot, made of top-class cinnabar clay, is plump and smooth-skinned, and shows a shiny scarlet luster, and on the base is stamped a seal "国良" (Guoliang).

壶等。1900 年为两广总督端方造壶，用印"陶斋""宝华庵"。民国四年（1915年）开始，俞国良为葛德和陶器公司、利用陶器公司制壶，他制作的四方传炉壶作为中国送展的紫砂器之一，于1933 年获美国芝加哥博览会优秀奖。

make a teapot at his home, the seal he used at the time included only one character "斋" (Studio). His works involved various styles, like *Hanjun* Teapot, *Ruding* Teapot, White Clay Teapot and so on. In 1900, Yu was commissioned by Duan Fang — governor of Guangdong and Guangxi — to make teapots, "陶 斋"

俞国良一生留下紫砂壶共60多把，名作有大中小各式传炉壶、线元壶、掇球壶、仿鼓壶、汉君壶、松竹梅壶、鱼化龙壶等。

> 裴石民

裴石民，出生于1892年，现代制壶名家。裴石民少年时师从陶瓷艺人江案卿学习陶艺，艺成后擅制仿古紫砂器，颇负盛名。裴石民技艺精湛，风格清秀典雅，既能做典雅脱俗的光素茗壶，又能做千姿

- **登科壶（裴石民制）**
  "登科"即中国古代科举考试时，高中进士，后来多用作结婚的祝福词或吉祥语。此壶的设计天然妙趣，造型别致。

  Dengke Teapot, by Pei Shimin

  Originally, *Dengke* meant that someone has passed the Imperial Examination. Later, this term was used as a blessing for marriage. This teapot is of natural design and unique shape.

(Pottery Studio) and "宝华庵" (Baohua Temple) being the seals used in this period. Since 1915, he began to make teapots for two pottery companies. The Square Furnace Teapot he made won a prize in the Chicago Exposition held in the United States in 1933.

Over his career Yu had made a total of more than 60 teapots, among which the small, medium and large-sized Furnace Teapots, *Xianyuan* Teapot, Ball Teapot, Drum-shaped Teapot, *Hanjun* Teapot, etc., are considered masterpieces.

> Pei Shimin

Pei Shimin, born in 1892, a famous teapot artist in modern times, was apprenticed to a potter at an early age. Pei was known to all for his emulation of ancient purple clay wares. He was reputed to have superior skills, and all of his works were elegant and refined in shape. He excelled at making smooth pots, sculpture pots as well as small plates, cups and cauldrons, which share the sedate, solid characteristics of bronze wares.

Pei Shimin's works were mostly small pieces, and were often made to recall archaic wares. The ingenious ideas and well-balanced design found in his

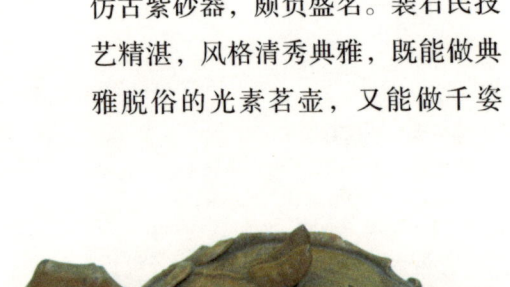

壶盖：壶盖采用嵌入式结构，与壶身浑然一体，口边有一圈线纹。壶盖上塑一枝桃树枝为纽，盖上亦塑三个小桃。

Lid: the lid is sunk into the lip of the opening and seamlessly integrated into the body. Around the opening is raised up a narrow band, on the lid the knob is designed to shape like branches of a peach tree, interspersed with three mini peaches.

印贴装饰：采用印贴技法做出"五福捧寿"的浮雕图案。于壶身一面贴塑桃树一枝，上有五个寿桃，又塑两只飞舞的蝙蝠；又于壶身另一面贴塑三只蝙蝠。

Decoration: bas-relief patterns are done on both sides of the body by means of printing and pasting. Two bats flying around a peach tree with five peaches on the one side, the other, three bats, symbolize good luck and longevity (the Chinese character "福" (luck) puns with "蝠" (bat), while peach normally stands for longevity).

壶嘴：三弯桃桩嘴。

Spout: the triple-curved spout is of the shape of the tree trunk.

壶把：卷曲桃枝把。

Handle: the handle is designed to shape like a curved branch.

- **五福蟠桃壶（裴石民制）**
  此壶身似桃形，泥色别致，寓意吉祥。
  Teapot of the Fruit of Eternal Life, by Pei Shimin
  In shape of peach, this teapot has unusual color and symbolizes auspiciousness.

百态的花货茶具，且擅制水丞、杯盘、炉鼎等器，造型典雅别致，具有青铜器敦厚稳重的特点。

裴石民的作品以中小件陶器为主，常借鉴古器造型，构思超凡，简繁匀称，在紫砂艺苑中独树一帜。他制作的仿真果品尤为出名，

works made him unique in the purple clay industry. Pei was particularly known for his emulation of fruit forms, which earned the reputation of "the second Chen Mingyuan". He was also said to have made lid or cup holders for certain purple clay antiques. Few of Pei's works came from his later years; typical pieces of this

有"陈鸣远第二"的美誉。他还曾为供春树瘿壶配盖，为项圣思桃杯配托。裴石民晚年的作品不多，主要有石瓢壶、牛盖莲子壶等，多钤"裴石民年七十六制"，盖内以小印标明制作时间。

period include Teapot of Stone Gourd Ladle, Lotus Seed Teapot, etc., most of which were stamped with the seal " 裴石民年七十六制 " (Made by Pei Shimin at the age of 76), while inside the lid were there small seals marking the date of manufacture.

> 王寅春

> Wang Yinchun (1897-1977)

王寅春（1897—1977），现代紫砂制壶大师。王寅春13岁时便开始学习紫砂陶艺，制壶技艺精湛，制作茶壶以多、快、好著称，擅制光货、花货，其作品造型雍容大方，风格独特，规矩挺括，光润和谐，口盖合缝严密。王寅春自行设计了

Wang Yinchun, a preeminent teapot artist in modern times, began to learn potting skills at the age of 13. Wang excelled in making smooth pots and sculpture pots. Generous grace, unique style, well balance, smoothness, and precisely-fitting lids are highlights of his styles. He designed by himself dozens

- **裙花提梁壶（王寅春制）**
  此壶的壶身上部为椭圆形，线条流畅，表面浑圆光洁，仅于肩部贴塑百结绳纹；下部处理成装饰性很强的裙花六瓣纹，壶也因此而得名。

  Upper Handle Teapot in the Shape of a Skirt, by Wang Yinchun
  The upper part of this teapot is half-ellipsoid with beautiful curves and lines, the smooth surface is decorated with nothing but a twisted twine tied around the middle in the style of low relief; the lower part is made to recall the skirt, with decorative patterns resembling the petals of water chestnut flower, hence its name.

- 红串盖壶（王寅春制）

此壶表面光润无瑕，壶身为圆柱形，平底，圆肩，直颈圆盖，桥形纽上置一活圆环，壶把折圆微方。

Red Teapot with Ringed Lid, by Wang Yinchun

This teapot, with an immaculate surface, is of cylindrical shape; starting from the short straight neck, the round curves extend all the way down to the flat base, on the domed circular lid lies the ringed knob in the shape of bridge.

五六十种新壶式，代表作有亚明方壶、元条壶、六方菱花壶、六方抽角壶、梅花周盘壶等。

王寅春制作紫砂壶以又多又快又好而著称，传世精品颇多，所制之壶被统称为"寅春壶"，壶上印有"寅春"印章，"寅春壶"深得紫砂壶爱好者的追捧，收藏价值极高。此外，王寅春还积极办班教学，传授紫砂壶艺，为紫砂工艺的发展作出了巨大的贡献。

of new teapot styles — Yaming Square Teapot, Yuantiao Teapot, the Teapot of Water Chestnut Flower, etc., are typical examples.

Wang was reputed to be fast and efficient in making teapots. As a result, a large number of his works are extant today, and they are collectively referred to as "Yinchun Teapot". These pieces, bearing the seal " 寅春 " (Yinchun), were of high artistic value and therefore much sought after by teapot lovers. In addition, Wang was active in holding training courses to impart his potting skills, making great contributions to the development of the art of purple clay.

> Zhu Kexin (1904-1986)

Zhu Kexin, a renowned teapot artist in modern times, became apprenticed to a potter when 14 years old. The Bamboo Trunk Teapot and Bamboo Trunk Cup he made in his twenties won a golden prize at the Chicago Exposition held in the United States. As a versatile artist, Zhu was particularly known for his chasing and kneading techniques as well as the capability of designing. He designed and crafted numerous groundbreaking

> 朱可心

朱可心（1904—1986），现代制壶名家。朱可心14岁时便随宜兴紫砂艺人汪生义学艺，二十多岁时，所制的竹节壶、竹节杯便在美国芝加哥博览会上获得了金奖。朱可心技艺全面，尤擅雕镂捏塑，设计能力强，先后设计了几十种紫砂壶造型，万寿壶、云玉壶、报春壶、碗梅壶、彩蝶壶、劲松壶、翠松壶、可心梨式壶、圆松竹梅、汉 new teapot styles, such as the "Longevity Teapot", "Spring-coming Teapot", "Colorful Butterfly Teapot", "Pine Tree Teapot", "Round Pine, Bamboo and Plum Teapot", etc.

On Zhu's works, "可心" (Kexin), "朱可心" (Zhu Kexin) or "凯长" (Kaichang) were often found stamped. The pieces bearing seals on both the base and the lid were among his proud works. Additionally, he had also used a four-character square seal that read "人生自荣" (the glory depends on yourself), and then any pot bearing this seal would be

- 碗灯壶（朱可心制）

  传统的碗灯壶本为光货，即以古代百姓常用的碗灯为形，整体呈饱满有力的圆球状。但朱可心把此壶制成花货，设计十分巧妙。

  Oil Lamp Teapot in the Shape of Bowl, by Zhu Kexin

  Originally, this kind of teapot was meant to imitate the bowl-shaped oil lamp used by ancients and usually appeared as a fully spherical bisque piece. This work, however, was made cleverly by Zhu Kexin into a sculpture pot.

- 紫砂报春壶（朱可心制）

  此壶以塑小型竹节的心形为壶体，用浮雕和点浆法做出苍劲挺拔的梅花老枝为流，梅花老枝上的嫩枝延伸到壶体上，开出朵朵梅花。

  Spring-coming Teapot, by Zhu Kexin

  The body of this teapot emulates certain parts of a bamboo twig; the spout, made by means of bas-relief and other special skills, is of the shape of a vigorous branch of the plum tree, from which the twigs extend to the body and send forth several plum blossoms.

扁壶等均是他的杰作。

他的作品印有"可心""朱可心""凯长",壶底、壶盖皆有印款者是其较精的作品。朱可心还用过一枚"人生自荣"四字方印,钤此印款的作品,属精品中的精品。20世纪80年代,中国掀起紫砂壶收藏热,朱可心作为花货素饰器的一代宗师,自然成了众人的焦点。有些人找各种借口要用他的印章,承诺卖一把壶分五成利给他。面对金钱的诱惑,朱可心一概严词拒绝。不是自己亲手制的壶,绝不盖上自己的章。

朱可心是一位不断进取的制壶艺人,他善于从自然及生活中汲取创作灵感,其作品洋溢着浓郁的时代气息,风格浑厚淳朴,法度合宜。此外,他还一手培养了诸多紫砂匠师,著名的有李碧芳、谢曼伦、许成权、汪寅仙等。

deemed the finest of all fine pieces. In the 1980s when a collection of purple clay pot became popular, Zhu, as a master of teapot, was naturally a favorite among collectors. Some teapot makers had tried unsuccessfully to borrow his fame by using his seals on their works as Zhu would not give up his integrity.

An aspiring potter, Zhu looked to daily life and nature to find his subject matter. His works were often brimmed with the rich flavor of the times with a vigorous, solemn style. He was also the tutor of several celebrated teapot artists; Li Bifang, Xie Manlun, Xu Chengquan, Wang Yinxian were a few of his disciples.

- 彩蝶壶(朱可心制)

此壶壶身造型浑厚淳朴,未有任何装饰,只是重点地刻画壶嘴、壶盖和壶纽。

Colorful Butterfly Teapot, by Zhu Kexin

The body of the teapot is simple and has no decoration, while the spout, the lid and the knob are elaborately designed and decorated.

> 顾景舟

顾景舟（1915—1996），中国工艺美术大师，被誉为"现代最杰出的紫砂壶艺巨匠""壶艺泰斗"。顾景舟年轻时跟其祖母邵氏学艺，20岁便小有名气，以擅制光素作品著称。顾景舟制壶极其严谨，个个要求质量上乘，不满意的就要毁掉。其作品线条流畅，结构严谨，手法细腻，规矩挺括，代表作有锦云如意壶、汉方壶、雪华壶等。他制的壶多次获国家质量评比金质奖，为海内外爱壶人士争相收藏。

顾景舟喜欢以艺会友，曾与著名画家韩美林、工艺美术大师张守智合作制壶，为紫砂壶的发展注入了现代美学概念，开创了紫砂壶造型的新境界。

> Gu Jingzhou (1915-1996)

Gu Jingzhou, the master of Chinese industrial art, was honored as the "Greatest Master of Teapot Art of Modern Times". Gu was apprenticed to his grandmother at an early age and was something of a celebrity in his 20s. He was renowned for his bisque wares. When making teapots, he followed very strict requirements and destroyed whichever he found unsatisfactory. His works boasted smooth lines, rigorous structure, delicate ways and well-balanced design. Some of his best works including the Teapot of Auspicious Cloud, Han Square Teapot, Snowflake Teapot were critically acclaimed and much sought after by collectors both at home and abroad.

In collaboration with such famous artists as Han Meilin, the famous painter, and Zhang Shouzhi, the master of industrial art, Gu brought modern

- 大石瓢壶（顾景舟制）

石瓢壶是曼生壶中的经典壶式，这件石瓢壶一面刻有几枝竹枝，另一面刻有铭文，典雅别致。

Teapot of Large Stone Gourd Ladle, by Gu Jingzhou

This teapot is among the classic style of Manshang Teapots. On one side are engraved a few branches of bamboo twigs, on the other are the inscriptions, which appear elegant and novel.

- 汉云壶（顾景舟制）

  此壶以圆形线条为主，肩部线条凸起，延伸至壶嘴，曲折中富有变化，柔美中带有韧劲，富有古朴典雅的艺术魅力。

  Hanyun Teapot, by Gu Jingzhou

  This teapot features various round curves-soft yet tough to make more variations; the shoulder and the belly are divided by a raised line, which extends to the spout, lending a simple and elegant note to the teapot.

- 紫砂僧帽壶（顾景舟制）

  此壶棱角硬朗，线条流畅，造型奇特，壶身为六边形，壶盖为五瓣莲花形，第六瓣的位置改为注形流。

  Monk Cap Teapot, by Gu Jingzhou

  This unique-shaped teapot has angular edges and corners; the body is of hexagonal shape with smooth lines, the lid looks somewhat like a lotus of five petals, and the vacancy is taken by the spout.

此外，顾景舟在培养紫砂人才方面也不遗余力，培养出了多位高级工艺美术师，为紫砂产业的繁荣和发展作出了突出的贡献。

同时，他还参与了宜兴地区多座古窑遗址的发掘工作，为紫砂陶的历史沿革、名人传记、古陶鉴定做了大量的研究和资料收集工作，先后发表了有关紫砂陶艺数十万字的论文，撰写了《宜兴紫砂珍赏》一书，为研究宜兴陶艺奠定了基础。顾景舟穷毕生精力钻研紫砂陶

aesthetics to teapot, creating new artistic styles for teapot shapes.

Besides, Gu was credited with cultivating a number of senior arts and craftspeople. The efforts he put into this contributed greatly to the prosperity and development of the purple clay industry.

Meanwhile, he had taken part in the excavation of several sites of ancient kilns in Yixing, undertaken a great deal of research on the history of purple clay wares and antique pottery identification, collected a large number of artists' biographies, and authored many essays

艺，不断进取，勇于创新，以博大的胸怀，精湛的技艺，在紫砂发展史上谱写了辉煌的篇章。

> 蒋蓉

蒋蓉（1919—2008），当代著名紫砂陶艺家、中国工艺美术大师，堪称当代的花货大家。蒋蓉出生于紫砂工艺世家，自幼习艺，擅于将动物、植物等的形态经过艺术的提炼、创造，运用到自己的作品之中，精于文房雅玩及壶类制作，作品以陈设观赏为主，兼有一定的实用功能。她还擅长运用紫泥、绿泥、红泥，调配成绚丽多彩的颜色，完美演绎出紫砂壶的色彩之美，使紫砂壶拥有一种雍容华贵的气象，热烈而不娇艳。

蒋蓉的一生共创作了200多个品种的精品紫砂壶和工艺品，代表作有荷花壶、牡丹壶、百果壶、荷叶壶、蛤蟆莲蓬壶、南瓜壶、西瓜壶、莲藕酒具、百寿树桩壶、玉兔拜月壶、菊蕊花蝶壶、肖形果品、双龙紫砂砚等。

on teapot art including the book *The Appreciation of Yixing Purple Clay Wares*, laying the foundation for the study of the development process. Almost all his life was devoted to the art of purple clay. His innovation and consummate skills as well as his broad mind write a glorious chapter in the history of purple clay.

> Jiang Rong (1919-2008)

Jiang Rong was an eminent artist of purple clay wares and a master of Chinese industrial art, and was particularly known for her sculpture pots. Jiang was born in a family of potters and began to learn potting skills at an early age. She was able to cleverly integrate the shapes of animals and plants with her works, and was skilled in making small wares and teapots. What's more, she was an expert on mixing clay materials of different colors. By skillfully using the mixtures, she was able to provide the teapots with gorgeous grace and warm floweriness.

Over her career, Jiang had made more than 200 pieces of artworks, among which the Lotus Teapot, Peony Teapot, Fruit Teapot, Melon Teapot, Loong Inkstone, etc., were typical examples.

- 紫砂茶叶茶具（蒋蓉制）

此壶塑盛开的荷花为壶身，塑蓬为盖，其上的莲子颗颗都能活动；壶盖上塑青蛙为纽，塑嫩荷卷叶为壶流，塑荷花枝干为壶把，又塑红菱、荸荠、白藕为壶的三脚，其形色之巧，宛若天成。

Purple Clay Tea Set, by Jiang Rong

This teapot is modeled on a blooming lotus flower; the lid, in the shape of a seedpod, is surmounted with a few movable lotus seeds and a frog-shaped knob; the spout is made to recall the furled leaf, and on the opposite side is a curved lotus stem acting as the handle, the body rests on three legs in shape of water chestnut, chufa and lotus root respectively, all of which look natural and lively.

- 荷叶壶（蒋蓉制）

此壶选用绿泥制作，色泽青中泛蓝，与荷叶之色颇为相似。

Lotus Leaf Teapot, by Jiang Rong

Made of green clay, this teapot shows a color of bluish green, rather similar to the true leaves.

形象逼真的"百果盘"

在某届广交会（中国进出口商品交易会）上，一位前来采购订货的港商在展览大厅中流连忘返。当他经过一只"百果盘"时，从盘中拿起一颗花生放入口中，不料牙被磕得生疼。他吐出后才发现，这只是一件紫砂肖形艺术品。这件惟妙惟肖的"百果盘"，正出自蒋蓉之手。

The Realistic "Fruits and Container"

This work is so lifelike that it is easily passed for the real. It is said that a Hongkong merchant at the Cantonfair, deceived by its appearance, picked up a peanut from the plate biting it and almost broke his teeth until as last he found it was nothing but an artwork. This masterpiece was made by Jiang Rong.

板栗 Chestnut
荸荠 Chufa
核桃 Walnut
乌菱 Water Chestnut
茨菰 Arrowhead
花生 Peanut
白果 Ginkgo
葵花子 Sunflower Seed
西瓜子 Watermelon Seed

- **紫砂百果盘（蒋蓉制）**
  此九件紫砂象果品皆以捏塑手法作成，瓜果斑纹粗犷细致，各有不同；所配的紫砂荷叶盘更衬托出内承九珍的惟妙惟肖，生趣盎然。

  Fruits and Container, by Jiang Rong
  The nine pieces of fruits in this plate are made by means of kneading. The veins on these fruits bear meticulous details; the plate is in the shape of a lotus leaf, further adding a vivid and lively note to the fruits.

> 徐氏兄弟

徐汉棠、徐秀棠两兄弟出生于紫砂陶艺世家，兄弟二人均是紫砂大家，但各有所长。兄长徐汉棠专长制壶，弟弟徐秀棠以雕塑、陶刻及对紫砂理论的研究名扬四海。

徐汉棠（1932—），现代制壶大师，中国工艺美术大师。徐汉棠师从顾景舟，为其第一个弟子。他制壶颇有天赋，基础扎实，既擅制

> The Xu Brothers (1932/1937-)

Xu Hantang and Xu Xiutang were born in a family of potters. Both were teapot masters but excelled in different fields. Hantang was good at making teapots while Xiutang was known to all for sculpture, pottery engraving as well as his study on purple clay theories.

Xu Hantang, a master of teapot and Chinese industrial art, was apprenticed to Gu Jingzhou. Gifted in making teapots, he was adept at emulating archaic wares and creating new ones. His works often featured unique shapes, natural and precise veins. He was particularly known

- **礼花提梁壶（徐汉棠制）**
  此壶装饰有大小不一的红球，红球上缀有白点，有如欢庆礼花，故名。
  Upper Handle Teapot with Fireworks Patterns, by Xu Hantang
  As the name suggests, this teapot is decorated with red ball patterns dotted by white specks, similar to fireworks.

- **冰纹石瓢壶（徐汉棠制）**
  此壶造型端庄大方，开片线条流畅。口盖两面调转，开片线条亦能连通。
  Stone Gourd Ladle Teapot with Crackled Ice Patterns, by Xu Hantang
  This teapot looks dignified and tasteful. The hacking on the lid and body presents smooth lines, which can be matched even if the lid is turned around.

盖纽：豹的卷毛作纽。
Knob: curly hair of the cat is used as the knob.

壶盖：壶盖塑成豹首，变形的两只兽眼分别置于壶口。
Lid: the lid is designed to be the head, the two eyes, somewhat deformed, look to the spout.

壶把：豹尾作壶把。
Handle: the tail of the leopard acts as the handle.

壶嘴：扁流自椭圆形体上自然挫出。
Spout: the flat spout grows naturally from the oblate body.

壶身：壶身饰羽翼。
Body: the body is decorated with abstract patterns to symbolize the wings of the beast.

- 云豹壶（徐秀棠制）

此壶用紫泥制作，色泽红润，用黑、红、黄泥点染斑纹，利用俏色的云斑和流动的装饰线纹。此壶创作的总体构思虽然是塑古兽之形，但在具体的表现手法上做了很多创新。比如壶身之形，强调兽体之形服从器用之形，对兽体的刻画不是强调"栩栩如生"，而是强调意境的传达和形体特征的个性化。

Clouded Leopard Teapot, by Xu Xiutang
This teapot, reddish in tone, with scattered black, red and yellow flecks, is made of *Zini*. The body is decorated with cloud patterns and flowing lines. While this teapot is generally intended to picture the legendary beast, it comes with many innovative specifics: the body, though shaped somewhat like a leopard, is designed to be functional, meant to deliver a spiritual likeness but not seek an exact copy of the beast.

仿古器形，也精于创作新壶，其壶造型独特，似冰如玉，纹理妙若天成，壶盖移位，线纹吻合。他还擅于制作各式微型小花盆，人称"汉棠盆"，为上海盆栽界所爱。

for his mini vases of various shapes, which were hailed as "Hantang Vase" and much favored by bonsai lovers.

By creating new techniques for the production of purple clay models and finding new ways to make the lid,

徐汉棠对于现代紫砂产业的发展作出了重要贡献。他不仅开创了紫砂模型生产的新工艺，发明了铁模压坯、石膏注浆等制作壶盖的新方法，而且参与主编了《紫砂陶器造型》一书，推广发扬了宜兴紫砂文化。

此外，徐汉棠擅长运用紫砂开片冰纹手法制壶，大量运用铺砂、调砂、礼花、边花、填花、嵌银丝等多种装饰手法，所制之壶精美绝伦，深得收藏者追捧。

徐秀棠（1937—），现代制壶名师、雕塑名家，中国工艺美术大师。徐秀棠青年时师从陶刻名家任淦庭，学习陶刻装饰技艺，后来还曾学过很长时间的泥塑。

徐秀棠在紫砂雕塑和紫砂壶制

Hantang made great contributions to the modern purple clay industry. He also coauthored a book *Shapes of Purple Clay Wares*, promoting the culture of Yixing purple clay.

In addition, Hantang was clever at hacking into his teapots. With such decorative methods as mixing and spreading of clay particles, appliqué, flower lacing and silver inlay widely adopted, his works were extremely exquisite and therefore much sought after by collectors.

Xu Xiutang was a celebrated artist of teapot and sculpturer as well as a master of Chinese industrial art. In his youth, Xiutang learned engraving and decorative skills after Ren Ganting — a famous artist of pottery engraving, and later he

- **大吉壶（徐秀棠制）**
  此壶用细润的紫砂泥制作，色泽红润坚致。壶身似"吉"字形，鼓腹、圆底、细颈，气势不凡。

  Good Luck Teapot, by Xu Xiutang
  This teapot is made of fine clay. Reddish in tone, it is suggestive of metals. The body, with a bulging belly, short neck and swelling base, looks somewhat like the Chinese character "吉" (meaning luck), presenting an extraordinary note.

作上造诣颇深,一生创作了大量紫砂雕塑和名壶,其作品采用色泥、镶嵌、琢毛等装饰手法,将紫砂工艺与中国书法、绘画联系起来,实现了传统技艺、文化和现代风格的完美结合,创造出别具一格的紫砂艺术。他的作品经常出新出奇,被誉为"天南独秀,一时无双"。

他还与顾景舟一起编辑《宜兴紫砂珍赏》,撰写了《紫砂陶刻艺术理论》等论文,成就非凡。

- 灵芝壶(徐秀棠制)
  此壶以紫泥制成,外形酷似灵芝,壶身与壶钮、壶把结合得非常完美。
  Glossy Ganoderma Teapot, by Xu Xiutang
  This teapot is made of *Zini* and shapes like glossy ganoderma, the body is perfectly compatible with the knob and handle.

devoted much time to clay sculpture.

Xiutang was quite accomplished in making purple clay sculptures and teapots, and he produced a great number of sculptures and teapots over his career. In his works decorative methods like colored clay, inlay and sgraffito, were always found used. By bringing together Chinese calligraphy, painting and purple clay skills, he integrated perfectly traditional techniques and culture with modern styles, creating a unique art of purple clay. His works often showed novelty and were hailed as "Incomparable at the Time."

He also co-worked with Gu Jingzhou on the book *The Appreciation of Yixing Purple Clay Wares* and authored many original essays, *Art Theory of Purple Clay Wares Engraving* being one example; all these embodied his extraordinary achievements.

> Li Changhong (1937-)

Li Changhong, a senior artist of industrial art, learned skills after Gu Jingzhou in his early years and mastered all the required techniques. Later, he continued to make explorations based on traditional shapes of purple clay wares, and strived

> 李昌鸿

李昌鸿（1937—），高级工艺美术师。李昌鸿早年师从顾景舟学艺，掌握了紫砂壶制作生产的全流程工艺。此后，他在继承紫砂传统造型的基础上，不断开拓创新，在 for serenity, fashion and elegance. As a reward for his efforts, Li finally achieved various new techniques, like "clay twisting decoration" and "pattern printing decoration".

Honest and modest, Li was a man of integrity. At his leisure, he was used to placing himself in calligraphy and

- 一粒珠壶（李昌鸿制）
  Bead Teapot, by Li Changhong

- 掇只壶（李昌鸿制）
  此壶造型润朴典雅，工艺技法高超。
  Ball Teapot, by Li Changhong
  This teapot is of simple and elegant shape and shows mellow luster, reflecting superior potting skills.

- 青玉四方壶（李昌鸿制）
  此壶借鉴中国传统的青铜器钟、鼎造型，在壶嘴、盖钮等处借鉴了中国传统的玉器造型，构思巧妙，文化底蕴深厚。
  Square Chime Teapot, by Li Changhong
  This teapot, incorporating ingenious ideas and rich cultural deposits, is made to recall traditional Chinese bell or cauldron, the spout and the knob are somewhat suggestive of traditional Chinese jade wares.

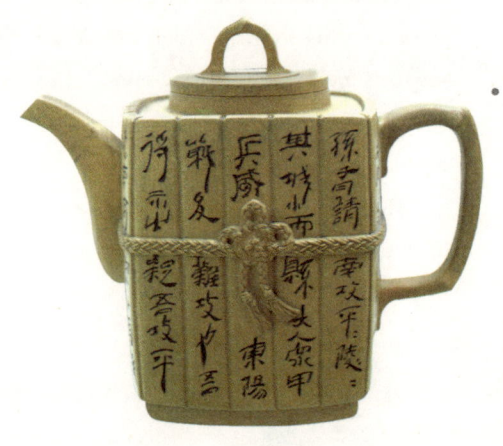

• **竹简壶（李昌鸿、沈蘧华制）**

此壶壶身为扁长方体，表面做成竹简之形，正背面各为五片竹简，左右面各为三片竹简，腰部有一束绳及绳结扣，竹简上刻有《孙子兵法》一篇。

Bamboo Slip Teapot, by Li Changhong and Shen Quhua

The body of this teapot is of flat cuboid shape modeled after a bundle of bamboo slips, with three pieces on the left and right side separately, five on the front and rear side respectively, which are held together by a twisted twine tied round the middle, on the bamboo slips is engraved an episode of *Sunzi's Art of War*.

造型设计、装饰方面力求寓意深邃、款式新颖、格调高雅，成功研发出"紫砂绞泥装饰""紫砂印纹装饰"等新装饰工艺。

李昌鸿为人敦厚诚恳，谦虚好学，艺德高尚，闲暇之时喜欢书法绘画，钻研紫砂理论，培育新人，传授技艺。除了创作紫砂壶，研究紫砂文化外，他还与顾景舟、徐秀棠合编了《宜兴紫砂珍赏》，并先后编写了多部书籍，发表了三十余篇有关紫砂艺术研究的论文，为推动宜兴紫砂文化的研究、紫砂产业的发展作出了重要的贡献。

他的作品多次在国内国际博览会上获奖，在紫砂行业内有"获奖

painting, studying purple clay theory and imparting his skills to young craftsmen. Besides making teapots and studying the culture of purple clay, he co-worked with Gu Jingzhou and Xu Xiutang on the book *The Appreciation of Yixing Purple Clay Warcs* and authored a number of books and published dozens of essays on purple clay art. Li made great contributions to the development of purple clay culture and industry.

His works won numerous awards both at home and abroad, and he was thus reputed as the "Trophy Hoarder" within the field. Among Li's many award-winning pieces, the "Bamboo Slip Tea Set" by him and Shen Quhua, won a golden prize in Leipzig International

大户"之称。其中，1984年与沈蘧华合作的"竹简茶具"荣获德国莱比锡国际博览会金质奖，这是当代紫砂作品首次在国际上荣获大奖。

> 李碧芳

李碧芳，出生于1939年，高级工艺美术师。李碧芳年少时师从朱可心，学习紫砂制陶技艺，基础扎实，制壶技艺十分全面，善于吸取各名家的长处，其作品涵盖了光

Exposition held in Germany in 1984. It is the first contemporary work of purple clay to have won an international award.

> Li Bifang

Li Bifang, born in 1939, was a senior artist of industrial art. She was apprenticed to Zhu Kexin in her early years and developed comprehensive potting skills. By drawing the essence of various masters, Li included smooth pot, sculpture pot and veined pot in her works and she was particularly remarkable for

- 圆韵壶（李碧芳制）
  此壶圆润光洁，造型古朴简洁。
  Round Teapot, by Li Bifang
  This teapot, full and plump, looks primitive and simple, and shows a bright and clean luster.

- 双龙戏碧壶（李碧芳制）
  Double Loongs Teapot, by Li Bifang

货、花货、筋囊货，其中尤以筋囊货见长。她的作品外形质朴，形态优雅，工艺精湛，表现出一种浓浓的书卷气息。

李碧芳在制壶之余，还致力于壶式创作和培育新人，多年来培训了大批艺徒，共计数百人。

her veined wares. Her works featured pristine nature, elegant shapes and excellent skills.

Besides making teapots, Li also went in for the creation of new styles of teapots and fostering young craftsmen, hundreds of apprentices contributed to her efforts over the years.

> 吕尧臣

吕尧臣（1941—），中国工艺美术大师。吕尧臣早年随制壶名家吴云根学习陶艺，后来又得到朱可心、顾景舟等大师的指点，制壶技艺突飞猛进，谙熟紫砂造型规律以及多种艺术处理手法。20世纪80年代开始，吕尧臣受聘于"中国宜兴

> Lv Yaochen (1941-)

Lv Yaochen, a master of Chinese industrial art, in his early years learned potting skills after Wu Yungen — the celebrated teapot artist; later he was given instructions by another two masters Zhu Kexin and Gu Jingzhou, and thus made big progress in making teapots. Lv, familiar with teapot shaping and various

- 伏羲壶（吕尧臣制）

伏羲壶为吕尧臣所创，选材用泥讲究，造型奇特，人称"尧臣壶"。

Fuxi Teapot, by Lv Yaochen (In Chinese Mythology, Fuxi Was the First of the Five Emperors of the Legendary Period)

The style of this teapot was invented by Lv Yaochen. Made of well-chosen clay material, this teapot is of the unique shape, neither flighty nor mighty, hence it is reputed as the "*Yaochen* Teapot".

- **玉带提梁壶（吕尧臣制）**

此壶壶身呈扁长方形，四角棱线挺拔，在壶体的两个长侧面模印有卷草纹；长方形壶足，提梁为平扁状，两端与壶肩等宽并浑然一体。

Jade Belt Teapot, by Lv Yaochen

This teapot is of squat rectangular shape, with the edges of the body extending firmly towards the oblong base; on the long sides of the body are engraved patterns of scroll design; the upper handle is of flat type, both ends of which are of equal width with the body.

陶瓷博物馆"，建立了吕尧臣陶艺工作室——醉陶居。

在钻研紫砂壶工艺的同时，吕尧臣还注重从古代陶器、青铜器、玉器、漆器等艺术品中吸取精华，丰富紫砂壶的壶式。他独创的"吕氏绞泥"装饰法（发明了绞泥装饰工艺），使作品出神入化，为他赢得了"壶艺魔术师"的美称。

吕尧臣的作品造型新颖别致，做工细腻严谨，整体比例恰当，风格韵秀古朴，意蕴深刻隽永，多次获得国内国际工艺美术大奖，具有极高的收藏价值。1992年，吕尧臣被列入英国剑桥大学编著的《世界名人录》。

decorative methods, was employed during the 1980s by China Yixing Ceramics Museum and established his potting studio — the *Zuitao* Studio.

Lv also gave great attention to absorbing the essence of archaic pottery, bronze, jade and lacquer wares, so he enriched the styles of teapots and created his way of twisting clay, thereby earning the reputation of "Teapot Magician".

Lv's works, incorporating novel shapes, fine workmanship, well balanced, pristine style and rich connotation, won numerous awards both at home and abroad, and enjoyed a very high collection value. In 1992, Lv Yaochen was included in "Who's Who in the World" compiled by the University of Cambridge.

> 汪寅仙

汪寅仙（1943—2018），中国工艺美术大师。汪寅仙出生于陶瓷世家，早年随制壶名家吴云根学习陶艺，后师从朱可心门下，还先后得到裴石民、王寅春、蒋蓉、顾景舟等名师的指导。

汪寅仙技术全面，技艺精湛，光货、筋囊货均有相当造诣，尤擅花货创作。她的作品惟妙惟肖、气韵生动，具有浓厚的中国传统艺术文化特色。

此外，她还熟知紫砂泥性，擅长调配泥色，并将抽象造型与自然相结合，突出作品造型特色及优雅

> Wang Yinxian (1943- 2018)

Born in a family of potters, Wang Yinxian was a master of Chinese industrial art. She was apprenticed to teapot artists Wu Yungen and Zhu Kexin in her youth and was also given instructions by various masters, such as Pei Shimin, Wang Yinchun, Jiang Rong, Gu Jingzhou.

Wang, a versatile and skillful artist, was quite accomplished in smooth pot and veined pot and above all things, in sculpture pot. Her works were vivid, lively and had distinctive characteristics of traditional Chinese art and culture.

Besides, she was quite familiar with the attributes of clay, and was good at mixing clays of different colors. Her large quantities of masterworks,

- **西瓜壶（汪寅仙制）**
此壶是典型的花货，以西瓜为形，上塑有西瓜的藤蔓，十分精致秀美。
Watermelon Teapot, by Wang Yinxian
This teapot, in the shape of watermelon, is a typical sculpture piece. The body is decorated with melon vines, which looks very delicate and beautiful.

• 神鸟出林壶（汪寅仙制）

此壶的壶嘴似鸟头，壶身以弧线构成，并以鸟儿振翅展翅的姿态构成提梁，犹如一只昂首翱翔的鸟儿，正在搏击云天。

Bird Teapot, by Wang Yinxian

This teapot is modeled in the shape of a flying bird, the spout is designed to be the head of the bird, from the spout there raises a curved handle delicately designed to recall the spreading wings.

的气韵，制作了大量的紫砂精品。

汪寅仙至今有作品数百件，其方器作品有龙凤印包壶、大印包壶等；光货和筋囊货讲究整体结构的缜密及线条流畅，以简练的形式表达紫砂壶特有的美感与深度，作品有曲壶（与张守智合作）、鱼龙壶、玉炉壶等；花货注重形象、神韵和气质的统一，诠释大自然旺盛的生命力和饱满盎然的生趣，作品有南瓜壶、梅桩壶等。

> 周桂珍

周桂珍（1943—），中国工艺美术大师。周桂珍曾先后拜名家王

cleverly integrating the abstract with natural shapes, were praised for their characteristic shapes and elegant notes.

Among Wang's hundreds of works, Loong and Phoenix Teapot in Shape of Wrapped Seal, Big Teapot in Shape of Wrapped Seal are among typical examples of square pieces; her smooth and veined pieces are represented by deliberate structure and smooth lines, achieving great effects through simple styles; major works of these categories include Curly Lines Teapot, Fish & Loong Teapot, Jade Stove Teapot, etc.; what sets her sculpture works apart is its lively appearance and natural interest, and Pumpkin Teapot, Plum Tree Teapot are good examples of this category.

• 集玉壶（周桂珍制）

此壶壶身圆润，壶嘴、壶把、壶盖和盖纽取自古玉器的造型和纹饰，故名集玉壶。为了突出古玉器的风貌，壶身上塑有一条凸弦纹，并在下方又加刻一条工整的阴线。

Jade Collecting Teapot, by Zhou Guizhen

This teapot is the shape of a round box, the spout, lid, handle and knob are designed to recall either the appearance or the patterns of archaic jade wares, hence its name. To highlight the style of archaic jade wares, around the body is placed a raised line, under which is further placed a thinner one.

• 北瓜提梁壶（周桂珍制）

此壶因壶身似瓜而得名，盖采用嵌盖式结构，形似瓜蒂及瓜头；提梁呈倭角长方形，表面光洁，仅上端有浮雕的瓜须；颈部装饰有葫芦花纹浮雕。

Pumpkin Teapot with Upper Handle, by Zhou Guizhen

This teapot looks like a pumpkin; the lid, embedded into the body, is shaped like the pedicle and head of the pumpkin; the handle, with a rectangular shape and rounded corners, is embossed with vines coiling around the upper part; the neck is decorated with gourd patterns in relief manner.

寅春、顾景舟为师学习制壶。在两位壶艺大家的指导下，周桂珍的紫砂壶制作技术进步很快，终成大器。

周桂珍设计制作的紫砂壶构思新颖，做工精细，造型简练，儒雅大度，意境深远，蕴含女性的秀丽与和美。许多艺术大师，如刘海粟、朱屺瞻、冯其庸等，都曾在周

> Zhou Guizhen (1943-)

Zhou Guizhen, a master of Chinese industrial art, learned skills after Wang Yinchun and Gu Jingzhou, and she was quick to learn under the guidance of these masters, eventually becoming an eminent artist.

竹提梁壶（周桂珍制）
Teapot with Bamboo-shaped Upper Handle, by Zhou Guizhen

Zhou's works come with novel ideas, fine workmanship, simple shapes and give exquisite refinement as well as feminine beauty. Many of the great artists, like Liu Haisu, Zhu Qizhan and Feng Qiyong, had dedicated poetry or paintings to her teapots. In 1978, the Jade Collecting Teapot, designed by Gao Haigeng and made by Zhou Guizhen, was selected as a national gift presented by Deng Xiaoping to Japanese leaders during his first visit to Japan.

> ## Gu Shaopei (1945-)

Gu Shaopei, a master of Chinese industrial art, began to learn potting skills at the age of 13, and was later given instructions by Gu Jingzhou — the teapot master, and he thus developed profound skills in making teapot.

A versatile artist, Gu excels in making teapots, basins, bottles and especially vases. His works, featuring simple, elegant and dignified style, as well as strong oriental and traditional flavor, won numerous awards both at home and abroad. In 1984 the "Longevity Vase" — a giant purple clay vase made by Gu — was awarded the golden prize in Leipzig International Exposition held

桂珍的壶上题诗作画。1978年，由高海庚设计、周桂珍制作的集玉壶被选为邓小平首次访问日本的国家礼品。

> ## 顾绍培

顾绍培（1945—），中国工艺美术大师。顾绍培13岁便开始学习紫砂陶艺，后又得名家顾景舟指点，制壶功力深厚。

顾绍培制陶技艺非常全面，能制作紫砂壶、盆、瓶，尤擅做紫砂

- 高风亮节茶具（顾绍培制）

这套紫砂茶具是方器造型与花塑器手法的结合，造型秀美典雅。茶壶的壶身为高四方直筒形，每面刻出四根成排的竹段，竹子的肌理特征刻画得十分生动，竹节、芽眼活灵活现。壶身中部又塑critique双竹枝环绕之态，竹枝上又生出一枝嫩竹叶，整体充满生机。

Tea Set in the Shape of Bamboo Sticks, by Gu Shaopei

This elegant tea set is square in section. Done in a sculpture manner, it is modeled in the shape of a bundle of bamboo sticks. With four pieces carved on each side, the sticks are held together by twisted bamboo twigs tied round the middle, from the twigs several tender bamboo leaves are growing out, vital and vigorous. The sticks are so realistically represented that some are even modeled with bud eyes.

- 天龙顶珠壶（顾绍培制）

此壶为典型的掇球壶，但壶身、器足、壶把均作特殊雕饰，以龙吐水顶珠为造型，立意新颖。

Pearl-over-water Teapot, by Gu Shaopei

This teapot is a typical example of a Ball Teapot. Special decorations are found on the body, handle and base: the handle is cleverly made to recall the loong, spouting water to support the pearl-like teapot body, which looks novel and imaginative.

花瓶，其作品精雅古朴、浑厚大方，具有东方美学的端庄和浓郁的传统文化气息，曾多次在国际、国内博览会上获奖。其中，特大紫砂"百寿瓶"曾在1984年德国莱比锡国际博览会上获得金奖。

除了进行紫砂器创作，顾绍培还从事紫砂教育和文化理论的研究，培养了大批紫砂制作人才，发表了多篇专业论文。顾绍培从38岁开始收徒，如今他的徒弟多数已成为高级工艺美术师。

in Germany.

Aside from making teapots, Gu is also engaged in the theoretical study of purple clay culture. He has trained a large number of craftsmen, most of whom are now senior artists of industrial art, and he also published many professional papers.